THE GREAT SEBASTIANS

THE
GREAT
SEBASTIANS

A Melodramatic Comedy

by

HOWARD LINDSAY *and* RUSSEL CROUSE

RANDOM HOUSE, NEW YORK

Photographs by Vandamm

To

ALFRED LUNT

and

LYNN FONTANNE

With admiration and affection

THE GREAT SEBASTIANS was first presented by Howard Lindsay and Russel Crouse at the Anta Theatre on the evening of January 4, 1956 with the following cast:

(IN ORDER OF APPEARANCE)

ESSIE SEBASTIAN	Lynn Fontanne
RUDI SEBASTIAN	Alfred Lunt
MANYA	Susan Frank
FIRST SECURITY POLICEMAN	Burns Oliver
SECOND SECURITY POLICEMAN	Martin Brandt
JOSEF	Arny Freeman
SERGEANT JAVORSKY	Simon Oakland
GENERAL OTOKAR ZANDEK	Ben Astar
FIRST SOLDIER	Peter Gumeny
SECOND SOLDIER	Michael Egan
VLASTA HABOVA	Peg Murray
COLONEL BRADACOVA	Anne Francine
SOPHIE CERNY	Eugenia Rawls
THIRD SOLDIER	Sheppard Kerman
KAREL CERNY	Jose Ruben
NOVOTNY	Grant Gordon
PAVLAT	Ben Hammer
DR. BALZAR	Edward Moor
MARIE BALZAR	Doris Fesette
BACILEK	Joseph Holland
CORPORAL	Ted Gunther

Directed by Bretaigne Windust

Settings by Raymond Sovey

Costumes by Main Bocher

Lighting by Jean Rosenthal

SCENES

The entire action of the play is laid in Prague, Czechoslovakia.
The time is March, 1948.

ACT ONE

Scene I. The stage of the Théâtre Variété.
(The scene starts just as the Great Sebastians have concluded their mind-reading act.)

Scene II. A combination sitting room and dressing room in the Théâtre Variété.
(The scene starts a few minutes before the end of Scene I.)

ACT TWO

The living room of General Zandek's home. The same night.

ACT THREE

The same as Act Two, one hour later.

CHARACTERS

(The situations and characters are entirely fictional.)

RUDI SEBASTIAN
ESSIE SEBASTIAN } *The Great Sebastians, a mind-reading act.*

MANYA: *A young woman with a determined and somewhat unpleasant devotion to her job, representative of the Cultural Action Committee for the Théâtre Variété.*

JOSEF: *The manager of the Théâtre Variété. A middle-aged man, nervous, frightened, distracted.*

GENERAL OTOKAR ZANDEK: *A man of great vitality, drive and cunning. He has a veneer of military efficiency but beneath it is the superstitious soul of the peasant.*

SERGEANT JAVORSKY: *A quietly alert and businesslike soldier. He is about forty years old.*

VLASTA HABOVA: *She is buxom, very female. As a girl she was a factory worker. She now has a high position in the Communist regime and thoroughly enjoys her change from "underdog" to "overbitch."*

JARKA BRADACOVA: *She is a large woman with the rank of Colonel on General Zandek's staff.*

SOPHIE CERNY: *She is a nervous, frightened, humorless woman of middle-age.*

MARIE BALZAR: *A very pretty and attractive, if brainless, young woman.*

KAREL CERNY: *He is an intellectual Communist. He went from the university faculty to a top job in the Party.*

PAVLAT: *He is a stocky, bald man of middle-age. He was a worker before his shrewdness promoted him to a position of importance in the Party.*

ZIKMUND NOVOTNY: *He is tall and dark, not without charm. A good politician.*

TANI BALZAR: *He is an attractive man in his early thirties, pleasant in manner and very much in love with his wife.*

STEPAN BACILEK: *He holds an important office in the Communist Party. He has the quiet authority of a man who is used to having his orders obeyed.*

(*There are also a Corporal, three Soldiers, and two members of the Security Police.*)

ACT ONE

ACT ONE

Scene I

The stage of the Théâtre Variété, Prague. It is an evening in March, 1948.

As the house lights dim out the house curtain rises and the orchestra plays fast "exit music." As the lights are thrown on, we see an olio drop, which is the background to a scene in "one."

The backdrop depicts a typical classic landscape in the style of the turn of the century—a columned terrace looking out on a moonlit lake and its surrounding mountains—encased in an elaborate, gold-painted rococo frame. All of this is on a pale blue background which, in turn, is framed by "theatre-red" swagged, velvet draperies, painted on the same drop.

The border and downstage wings are painted as a grand drape, in the same red, which is swagged and partly conceals two painted marble columns on either side. These in turn contain lighted frames, each holding a large card which reads, THE GREAT SEBASTIANS.

On stage, center, is an armchair which is probably known in the property room as the "throne chair." It is a high-backed, ornate gilt chair, upholstered in red velvet with an elaborate gold appliquéd design. Downstage right are steps leading down into the audience.

To the noisy excitement of the music, the SEBASTIANS *enter briskly from the right,* MADAME SEBASTIAN *first.* MADAME *is in a white flowing chiffon robe and a bejeweled turban, all of somewhat Oriental design.* SEBASTIAN *is in old-fashioned and well-worn dress clothes with tails. His outsized shirt studs bear the letter* S.

They acknowledge the applause of the audience with bows and smiles and exit, SEBASTIAN *allowing* MADAME *to exit first. This entrance and exit is repeated twice, all of which should convey to the audience that the* SEBASTIANS *are taking bows at the conclusion of their act.*

On the third entrance SEBASTIAN *holds up his hand, the orchestra stops playing, the applause ends and he has the attention of the audience.*

3

THE GREAT SEBASTIANS

SEBASTIAN

(Crossing to below throne chair, ESSIE following,
holding his right hand)
Ladies and Gentlemen—may I thank you for the way in which you
have received our act. Our sole purpose has been to mystify and
amuse you—and I must say, in all our experience, you have been the
greatest audience that we have ever played to! *(Turning to ESSIE for*
confirmation) Isn't that so, Madame?

ESSIE

(With a flourish of her right hand)
Oh, you were marvelous!
　　(ESSIE is cockney and whenever they are in their act, her cockney
　　accent is rather elegant.)

SEBASTIAN

During our engagement here in Czechoslovakia, every audience
has been so inspiring—but tonight there has been an excitement. . . !
Perhaps it is because you know this is our farewell performance in
Czechoslovakia—or perhaps it is because this is Prague, the city of my
birth.
　　(The orchestra strikes up three and a half bars of the Czech
　　national anthem. SEBASTIAN stands at attention.)

ESSIE

We hate to leave you but from here we go to London—the city of
my birth. *(The orchestra strikes up eight bars of "Britannia Rules*
the Waves." ESSIE and SEBASTIAN come to attention, and ESSIE salutes.
As the music ends, she bows to the conductor in the pit) Thank you,
Miroslav.

SEBASTIAN

From London, we start our grand tour—Germany—*(The orchestra*
starts "Die Wacht am Rhein." SEBASTIAN quickly gestures, the orches-
tra stops, and he continues)—France, Italy—and in every country,
we do the act in the native tongue.

4

THE GREAT SEBASTIANS

ESSIE

We're the only act ever to read minds in five different languages.

SEBASTIAN

In England we do the act in English—just as at this moment we are
addressing you in Czech. Oh, you have been so wonderful—we could
go on playing to you forever!

ESSIE

(*Leading* SEBASTIAN *to the right*)
Yes, but I'm sure you want to see the rest of the bill.

SEBASTIAN

(*Pulling her back toward the center*)
It has been such a great pleasure—

ESSIE

(*Interrupting*)
The next act is one of the most remarkable animal acts that I have
ever seen.
(*Starting toward the right again.*)

SEBASTIAN

(*Unhappily*)
Yes. Fink's Mules. (*Resigning*) Well, good-bye—

ESSIE

Au revoir—

SEBASTIAN

Auf Wiedersehen—

ESSIE

Till we meet again—

ESSIE and SEBASTIAN

—And God . . . bless . . . you!
(*The orchestra starts up the "exit music," the* SEBASTIANS *gesture lavishly to the audience and exit, right. The audience ap-
plauds again.* SEBASTIAN *returns alone to take another bow.*)

5

SEBASTIAN
(*Throwing up his hand, which stops the music and applause*)
Ladies and Gentlemen—(*Coaxing audience*)—does that mean you want to see some *more* of our act? (*Applause again;* SEBASTIAN *reaches offstage for* ESSIE's *hand, braces himself and tugs, and the reluctant* ESSIE *enters once more*) You have been so magnificent—we can't deny you—

ESSIE
(*With forced laughter*)
Well, good night again.
(*She bows, starts off;* SEBASTIAN *holds her firmly.*)

SEBASTIAN
Surely, Madame! (*More forced, polite laughter from* ESSIE) How can we refuse these wonderful people? (*She gives in, and he leads her to the throne chair*) Let's see, what can we do? I know. (*He seats* ESSIE *and starts to blindfold her with a large black satin blindfold which he takes from the back of the chair*) This time I shall blindfold Madame and come down among you, and try to send back to her across the intervening space the thoughts you put into my mind. (*Having finished blindfolding* ESSIE, *he leans with his elbows across the back of the chair*) Remember, the little lady makes no claim to occult or supernatural powers. (*Crossing to the steps leading to the audience*) However, if you believe that what you see is caused by odic force, psychometry, metaphysical manifestation or the simple triumph of mind over matter, you are at liberty to do so. And may I add, we have performed before all the leading scientists of every country in which we have appeared—and Madame has amazed them all.

ESSIE
I even amaze myself.

SEBASTIAN
(*Pausing at the top of the steps*)
Madame, are you completely blindfolded?

ESSIE
Yes.

6

SEBASTIAN

Can you swear to this audience that you cannot see?

ESSIE

I see only with the inner mind.

SEBASTIAN

(*Going down the steps into the audience, as the house lights come up to full, and the orchestra starts to play very softly, "The Skaters' Waltz"*)

Madame, I am now going down into the audience. Let your mind be a blank, ready to receive the impressions that will vibrate toward you from where I stand. . . .

SEBASTIAN

Madame, I am at the side of a gentleman in the—(*He counts the rows*) second row. (*Note: It has been rumored that* SEBASTIAN *always knew the name of a member of the audience*) Does the image of this gentleman's name reach you?

ESSIE

It's not very clear—I see an "M"—and an "E" . . . These seem to stand out as the initials.

SEBASTIAN

(*Leaning over the gentleman*)

Is that correct, sir? Are they your initials?

GENTLEMAN

Yes.

SEBASTIAN

(*Half turning back to* ESSIE)

Yes, Madame, that is correct! Perhaps you can tell me this gentleman's last name?

ESSIE

(*As* SEBASTIAN *snaps his fingers*)

"E" . . . "E" . . . It's not very clear . . . I have the impression the gentleman doesn't want us to know his last name.

7

THE GREAT SEBASTIANS

SEBASTIAN

(*Moving on*)
We will move on. (*He sights a handbag, holds it up*) And now, Madame?

ESSIE

It's—a handbag.

SEBASTIAN

But the color?

ESSIE

Black.

SEBASTIAN

(*Handing the handbag back to the owner*)
That is correct, Madame!

SEBASTIAN

(*Spotting a lady's wrist watch, holding up her wrist for the audience to see the watch as he points to it*)
Madame, can you tell me what this is?

ESSIE

It's round—it's flat—it's metal—something inside it moves—It's a watch—a wrist watch! A *lady's* wrist watch!

SEBASTIAN

Right!

ESSIE

—It was given to her as a present.

SEBASTIAN

(*To the* LADY)
Is that true, Madame?

LADY

—No!

SEBASTIAN

That's what I call a dirty trick. (*Calling back to* ESSIE) You are right, Madame, she gave it to herself. (SEBASTIAN *now looks toward the back of the house where there is a* GENTLEMAN, *holding up a key*) Madame, there is a gentleman at the back of the theatre. He is holding up something—can you tell me what it is? Quickly, Madame, quickly!

ESSIE

It's—a—it's a—

SEBASTIAN

Quickly! Quickly!

ESSIE

It's a—a—I'm afraid the gentleman isn't concentrating very hard—

SEBASTIAN

(*To the* GENTLEMAN)

Madame says you are not concentrating, sir, I'm sorry—you must have a very weak mind . . . (*He sights a fur coat, lifts it in the air*) Now, Madame, can you tell me what this is!

ESSIE

A fur coat!

SEBASTIAN

Right! Can you tell me what *kind* of fur?

ESSIE

I can—but I'd better not.

SEBASTIAN

(*Spying a bald head, holding his right hand over it*)

Madame, my right hand—what am I holding?

ESSIE

A billiard ball!

9

THE GREAT SEBASTIANS

SEBASTIAN

*(Spotting as blonde a blonde as he can find, putting
left hand on her head)*

My left hand, Madame—what am I touching? Think hard—concentrate—

ESSIE

A lady's head!

SEBASTIAN

Can you tell me the color of her hair?

ESSIE

Tonight—it's blonde!

*(The orchestra hits a flourish and goes immediately into the
"exit music" as* SEBASTIAN *dashes up the steps and* ESSIE *whips
off her blindfold, rises, crosses to right and exits.* SEBASTIAN,
who has allowed ESSIE *to cross in front of him, waves a last
farewell to the audience and, as the cards at either side of the
proscenium change to "*FINK'S MULES,*" he leans around the
edge of the wings, points to the sign and, trailing his hand
away, exits off right as*

The Curtain Falls

Scene II

A combined dressing room and sitting room in the Théâtre Variété, Prague.

The set is divided by a wall right of center. There is a door in this wall section leading from the sitting room into the dressing room. There is in the dressing room a curtained-off alcove, up left center, where a person can change clothes without being seen by the audience. The entrance from the stage is into the sitting room, down right.

The wainscoting woodwork of these rooms indicates that the theatre has seen many years.

The walls of the sitting room are in paneled sections of musty blue brocade. Right of the rear wall there is a small octagonally angled wall which houses a wood and marble imitation Adam fireplace, then angles again into the larger wall, stage right. A straight Empire chair stands against the wall between the fireplace and the door leading off, right. In the center of the sitting room there are a small round Beidermeier table and two chairs.

The upstage wall of the dressing room houses in its center a recessed open closet with a high shelf. On the shelf are a worn leather hatbox, an old leather suitcase and valise and two cardboard dress boxes, one on top of the other. Below the shelf various clothes hang on hooks. To the right of the closet and just below it is an old black wardrobe trunk, standing open. To the left of the clothes and also in the recessed area is a makeshift make-up table, actually a white wooden kitchen table, which is used by ESSIE SEBASTIAN. The table holds her various make-up equipment and also a theatrical mirror, gilt-framed, with green-shaded lights in its frame. This rests on the rear edge of the table and leans against the wall of the closet. At the dressing table there is a revolving stool covered and draped to the floor in chintz.

A little to the left of the recessed area, the wall again angles octagonally down left, corresponding to the angled section in the sitting room, then angles once more into the stage left wall of the dressing room. The small angled section this time houses the chintz-

11

curtained entrance to the offstage dressing area. Below and to the left of this entrance, a make-up shelf extends almost entirely across the left wall. The shelf, draped to the floor in the same chintz as the stool and alcove entrance, holds all of RUDI SEBASTIAN'S *make-up articles; flush with the shelf but bolted above it to the wall are two giant theatrical make-up mirrors, twice as large as the one on* ESSIE'S *table, both of which are also gilt-framed and have in their frames green-shaded light bulbs. At the make-up shelf there are two bent-wood chairs, one before each mirror. Below the door and its section of wall, up center, is an old theatrical wicker basket facing left with the letters* G.S. *painted in black on the downstage end.*

The walls of the dressing room area are painted a musty gray-brown.

AT RISE: MANYA, *a girl in her middle twenties, the theatre's representative on the Cultural Action Committee, is searching the ward-robe trunk.*

Two men, members of the Security Police, are also searching. The first is kneeling, looking in the hamper while the second is examining a make-up box on ESSIE'S *dressing table.*

We hear faintly the music of "The Skaters' Waltz" off right, since the scene commences a few minutes before the end of Scene I.

MANYA

(*Crossing to* FIRST SECURITY POLICEMAN)

Look over there! And hurry!

(*She indicates the dressing table down left and crosses to the*) hamper. JOSEF, *the manager of the theatre, enters the sitting room and, hearing the commotion, crosses into the dressing room.*)

JOSEF

What's that about? What are you doing?

(*The* SECOND SECURITY POLICEMAN *looks into, then exits into the dressing alcove.*)

MANYA

I'm having the room searched.

JOSEF

See here! I'm the manager of this theatre. And when you want to—

MANYA

(*Interrupting*)

Now you listen to me! These Sebastians have been in the country all this time. You know what their salaries are. And how much do you think they've given to the Cultural Action Committee?

JOSEF

Twenty-five per cent, of course.

MANYA

Not even five per cent! (*Applause is heard off right.* MANYA *goes to the* FIRST SECURITY POLICEMAN) They'll be coming. You'd better go. (*She crosses to the alcove, calls off through curtains*) Mirko!
(*The* SECOND SECURITY POLICEMAN *enters from the alcove and both* SECURITY POLICEMEN *cross into the sitting room and exit.* MANYA *follows them to the dressing-room door.*)

JOSEF

You can't expect the Sebastians to feel about the country the way we feel.

MANYA

(*Turning to him*)

I'll tell you what I feel—I feel they're trying to smuggle their money out of the country—those—those Westerners! (*She goes into the sitting room*) Bourgeois!
(*The "exit music" is heard, then the orchestra goes into the "Fink's Mules" music, off.*)

JOSEF

(*Following* MANYA)

You go slow! They are very well liked here.

13

MANYA

By whom?
(*She slouches into a chair.*)

JOSEF

By many people. The night they opened here, this room was filled with flowers. And who do you think sent most of them? Jan Masaryk.

MANYA

In some ways Masaryk is a fool.

JOSEF
(*Looking about apprehensively*)

Shhhh . . .

MANYA

He likes theatre people. What can he see in theatre people?

JOSEF
(*Indignant*)

I am theatre people. —And I like the Sebastians. (*Shakes his head*) But I *am* glad this is their last night.

MANYA

So am I. They haven't any sense of patriotism.

JOSEF

They haven't any sense. They don't know enough about politics to know who not to offend. This is the last time I book a foreign act.

MANYA
(*Rising*)

Good.

JOSEF

We'll just have to put up with our own entertainment. (*Looking off right*) They're coming! You'd better go!

MANYA
(Seeing ESSIE *approaching, off right)*
Madame Sebastian— (MANYA *goes off right as* ESSIE *sweeps past her, holding her dress up above her knees;* MANYA *re-enters, following* ESSIE *to the dressing-room door.)* I am here to get a contribution for the Cultural Action Committee, and I'm not going to leave until I—

ESSIE
(Angrily entering the dressing room)
Come back later!
(She slams the door in MANYA'S *face, crosses to stool and begins putting her turban, which she has just taken off, into a hatbox.* SEBASTIAN, *just as angry as* ESSIE, *enters, down right, and strides to dressing room as he takes off his coat.)*

JOSEF
Sebastian, if I may have a moment of your time—

SEBASTIAN
Come back later!
(He enters the dressing room and slams the door.)

JOSEF
(To MANYA)
We'll come back later. And let me give them their salary before you try to take it away from them!
(He and MANYA *exit.* SEBASTIAN *unzips* ESSIE'S *gown, turns and hangs his coat on a coat hanger which is on the hamper.)*

ESSIE
(Turning and looking at him)
I'm surprised to see you here. I thought you were still out there doing a single.

SEBASTIAN
(As he hangs the hanger on a hook which is on the doorjamb, up center, and fastens the coattails up with clothespins)
Unless you learn the new code, that's exactly what I will be doing —a single.

ESSIE

(*Stepping out of her gown*)

There's one thing you've never learned and it's about time you did. Always leave an audience wanting more.

SEBASTIAN

They were wonderful. They didn't miss a trick. They wanted more.

ESSIE

(*Hanging her dress on a hanger*)

Not by the time we finished with them they didn't. They were jolly well glad to be rid of us.

SEBASTIAN

Huh.

(*He crosses to the dressing table and sits.*)

ESSIE

You give too much. The Great Alexander said, "A good performer always leaves an audience hungry."

SEBASTIAN

(*Taking off his tie*)

If you mention the Great Alexander once more—

ESSIE

Now look, Rudi. Our act is supposed to last twenty minutes. It says so in the contract. Why do you want to give them half again as much for nothing? It's not good business.

SEBASTIAN

It's good business to know what we're doing out there.

ESSIE

I only missed once.

16

SEBASTIAN

You missed three times.

ESSIE

What three did I miss?

SEBASTIAN

I'll tell you. Madame—if you please—

ESSIE

Necktie.

SEBASTIAN

No! That's the old code. It's rubber boots. Now, Madame, if you please—

ESSIE

Rubber boots.
(*She goes into the alcove carrying her dress.*)

SEBASTIAN

Madame, if you please—

ESSIE
(*Off*)

Rubber boots.

SEBASTIAN

Madame, if you please—

ESSIE
(*Off*)

Rubber boots.

SEBASTIAN

If you please—

ESSIE
(*Off*)
Rubber boots. All right, all right.
(**SEBASTIAN** *rises and takes his tie box to the hamper.*)

SEBASTIAN

Now, Madame. There is a gentleman in the back of the theatre. He is holding up something. Can you tell me what it is? Quickly, Madame, quickly!

ESSIE
(*Off*)

No. You tell me.

SEBASTIAN

"Quickly" is key! Key—K-E-Y. Now Madame, quickly!

ESSIE
(*Off*)

Key.

SEBASTIAN

Quickly!

ESSIE
(*Off*)

Key.

SEBASTIAN

Quickly!

ESSIE
(*Off*)

Key. I know it now.

SEBASTIAN

Well, you didn't know it out there. (*He crosses back to the dressing table and sits. He removes his collar*) Now, Madame, can you name this?

ESSIE
(*Off*)

A scarf.

SEBASTIAN

No, Essie, no! That's the old code again. It's a fountain pen.
(ESSIE *enters in an old dressing gown.*)

ESSIE

Why do we have to change the old code? I did it for five years with
Alexander—then after I taught you, we've done it for twenty years.
Why do we have to change it now?

SEBASTIAN

(*As he takes off his shoes and gets into his slippers*)
Because if we'd gone on using the old code much longer the audience would have begun reading our minds. They're catching on.

ESSIE

(*Sitting at her dressing table*)
The bright ones know it's a trick. They're not going to stop to
figure it out.

SEBASTIAN

We should have changed it five years ago. You're not out in the
audience—working the aisles. You can't hear them whispering.

ESSIE

(*Packing small things on her dressing table in a make-up box*)
Look at the money it's cost us. Bang went our Edie's wedding present when we had to lay off for six months just to practice it.

SEBASTIAN

Well, we're going on practicing it. (ESSIE *rises during his speech,
puts her make-up towels in a trunk drawer*) Now, Madame, without
hesitation—

ESSIE

Rudi, where do we go from London?

SEBASTIAN

Munich. Now, Madame, don't hesitate.

ESSIE

Where? —Munich! Oh, Rudi, lovely! You go over very big in Munich, remember?

SEBASTIAN

Yes! They've got a good critic in Munich. (*He rises, takes shoes to hamper*) He called me the Swallow-tailed Swami! You can't ask for more than that.

ESSIE

Well, why not? You were sensational! Electric!

SEBASTIAN

Yes, I was good, wasn't I? You were good, too.

ESSIE

Thank you!

SEBASTIAN

So quick!

ESSIE

Thank you again!
(*She goes back up to her dressing table and sits.*)

SEBASTIAN

You seemed to have the answers before I even asked the questions. You know in Munich I could have sworn you were really reading minds. Oh, Essie, in Munich you were wunderschön! (*He holds out his arms and they embrace*) *In München warst du doch so schön, als wir uns liebten—ungeseh'n!* . . .

ESSIE

(*Speaking over his shoulder*)
Ja, ja, ja. Aber, in Munich we used the old code.
(SEBASTIAN *breaks away from her.*)

SEBASTIAN

(*Emphatically*)

We are using the new one, now. Now, Madame, without hesitation— (*She looks at him knowingly*) Don't hesitate— (*She continues to stare at him. He speaks sharply*) Madame, don't hesitate— (*She doesn't speak*) You see, you don't know it!

ESSIE

I do know it. Teeth! And we'll never use it till the day we die.

SEBASTIAN

Essie, remember that matinee when I caught a glimpse of an upper plate in a woman's handbag? It was you who said we should have a code word for teeth. I remember your very words. You said, "We'd have got the biggest laugh we ever got and the woman would have fainted."

ESSIE

And we haven't seen a tooth since.

SEBASTIAN

That's not the point. (*He goes to his table and sits*) Now, Madame, would you care to—

ESSIE

November. Rudi, for Heaven's sake.
    (*She is packing things on her table again.*)

SEBASTIAN

I can't hear you. Madame, would you care to—?

ESSIE

November. (*Slamming a box down on the table*) It's not as good as the old code!

SEBASTIAN

(*Shocked*)

How can you say that? I've been working on this code for two years. How can you compare it to that kindergarten system of Alexander's?

ESSIE

(*Crossing down to him*)

Alexander was the greatest mind reader that ever lived!

SEBASTIAN

(*Rising*)

If you please!

ESSIE

Rubber boots!

SEBASTIAN

(*Sitting down slowly*)

No, I don't mean that. I mean I don't want to hear any more about your first husband, if you please.

ESSIE

Rudi, if there hadn't been a Great Alexander, there could never have been a Great Sebastian. You know that.

(*She leans over him affectionately, rubs her cheek against his.*)

SEBASTIAN

Well, never mind. Now—

ESSIE

Now which? If it's "Now, Madame," it's handbag; if it's "Now, Essie," you're going to be nasty.

SEBASTIAN

Look, Essie, we came all the way to Czechoslovakia to break in the new code.

ESSIE

We came all the way to Czechoslovakia so that you could take a few bows.

SEBASTIAN

Bows! Me take bows?
(*He rises, crosses to the hamper with his hand mirror and towels.*)

ESSIE

Well, why not? (*Following him*) It's your country; you worked hard enough all through the war broadcasting back here, keeping their spirits up. They were proud of you, and they should be. I was proud of you then. I'm proud of you now.
(*She unfastens his waistcoat from behind.*)

SEBASTIAN
(*He beams*)

Are you?

ESSIE

Yes. You've had a good three months of showing off and you've enjoyed every minute of it.
(*She slaps him playfully on the seat of his pants.*)

SEBASTIAN
(*Turning to her*)
Showing off? Did I understand you correctly?

ESSIE

Cigar case.

SEBASTIAN

No, Essie, no! That's the old code again! (ESSIE *crosses to the laundry bag hanging downstage of the alcove door frame, and starts picking up soiled clothes from the floor and putting them in the bag*) Now you stop whatever you're doing, and we're going to rehearse—

ESSIE

Oh, no, we're not. We're going to finish packing up here and beat it to the nearest restaurant. I'm so hungry I could faint.

SEBASTIAN

Whose idea was it for us not to have any dinner?

ESSIE

Well, Mr. Masaryk gave us such an enormous lunch, I felt I couldn't eat again so soon.

SEBASTIAN

And you felt you'd save a few pennies.

ESSIE

Yes, I did. But I made a mistake because I've worked up the most expensive appetite.
(She crosses to the hamper with the laundry bag. JOSEF enters the sitting room, and goes to the dressing-room door.)

SEBASTIAN

Before you eat we're going to rehearse and we're going on rehearsing—Now, Madame, this object—
(JOSEF knocks at the center door.)

SEBASTIAN
(Crosses to center door, opens it)
Oh, it's you, Josef.

JOSEF

You told me to come back later.

SEBASTIAN

Well, then, come back later. *(Closing door, turning back to ESSIE)* Now, Madame, this object—

JOSEF
(Calling through door)

I have your salary!

ESSIE

Salary! . . .

SEBASTIAN

I suppose that money is more important to you than the act.

ESSIE

Yes.

SEBASTIAN
(As he crosses down to his dressing table and sits)
Oh, may God not strike you dead!

ESSIE

Come in, Joey.
(JOSEF enters with a pay envelope; ESSIE straightens up in time to snatch it out of his hand and slip it in her pocket.)

JOSEF

You two must be very happy. I had a brilliant audience for you tonight.

SEBASTIAN

You had a brilliant audience for us! I suppose the fact that we were playing here came as a complete surprise to them!

ESSIE

I suppose we broke the house record because you were the manager!
(She goes to her table and sits.)

JOSEF

Oh, no—I admit you had something to do with it.

SEBASTIAN

Something to do with it! Do you happen to know we broke the house record at the Palladium in London?

ESSIE

A much bigger theatre than this.

JOSEF

But, Sebastian—it was a very distinguished audience tonight.

SEBASTIAN

Well, I'll say this for them—they were a very easy audience. (*He rises, goes to the trunk with a towel full of make-up articles*) They were all Uncle Michaels.

JOSEF

Uncle Michaels?

ESSIE

Yes. Rudi has an Uncle Michael. He loves to have us read his mind. He believes every word we tell him.

SEBASTIAN

Josef, you're supposed to tell us whenever there's someone important out front. Who was the general in the third row tonight?

JOSEF

Sebastian—when you came for this week's return engagement I told you—government officials in the audience—do not call attention to them. This is a popular front government—it's very unpopular. Between six weeks ago and now it's entirely different.

SEBASTIAN

What's different about it?

THE GREAT SEBASTIANS

JOSEF

Sebastian, where were you week before last?

ESSIE

Karlsbad. One week.

SEBASTIAN

We broke the house record in Karlsbad, too.

JOSEF

Sebastian, that week you were in Karlsbad, the government of Czechoslovakia changed!

SEBASTIAN

Yes, we know, we know. And so it will change back again at the next election.
(*He goes back to his table and sits.*)

JOSEF

If there is a next election! Sebastian, you haven't been in Czechoslovakia for ten years. This is not 1938—this is 1948!

SEBASTIAN

Who was the general in the third row tonight—?

JOSEF

This government is Communist! It's the kind that will re-elect itself! (*He gasps, frightened*) I didn't say that! Remember, now, I didn't say that!
(*He hurries to center door, opens it, looks out cautiously, then closes it.*)

ESSIE

Joey, each time we come to this theatre you get more and more nervous. I don't believe you sleep well.

SEBASTIAN

Josef, who was the general in the third row tonight?

JOSEF

(*Crosses down to the hamper and sits*)
Monday night, when the Prime Minister was here, you mentioned his wife's birthday. (ESSIE *and* SEBASTIAN *chuckle at this*) And the year! She didn't like it. I thought sure the theatre was going to be closed. That night I didn't sleep for two nights.

ESSIE

(*Going to* JOSEF)
Joey, do they sell something here in Czechoslovakia—? In England we call it Ovaltine . . .
(*She sits on the hamper beside him.*)

SEBASTIAN

Josef, who was the general in the third row tonight!!

JOSEF

Well, I can tell you, now. It was General Zandek.

SEBASTIAN

You can tell us now!

ESSIE

General Zandek! Rudi, we have tons of information on General Zandek!
(SEBASTIAN *picks up a collar box on his table and hands it to* ESSIE.)

SEBASTIAN

Yes, get it out for me—it's in the third collar. (ESSIE *takes a turn-down collar from the collar box and, opening it, takes out a narrow strip of yellow paper on which is written information about* GENERAL ZANDEK) Josef, what makes us the great act that we are? It's because we read the minds of famous people—Gasperi, Churchill, DeGaulle. We tell them things about themselves that they've forgotten. That's how we prove to an audience we don't use confederates!

THE GREAT SEBASTIANS

ESSIE

Josef, remember our opening night here six weeks ago?

SEBASTIAN

We were sensational!
(ESSIE *hands* SEBASTIAN *the yellow strip of paper.*)

JOSEF

That was six weeks ago!

ESSIE

Three cabinet ministers.

SEBASTIAN

Clementis, Nosek, Kopecky!

ESSIE

I got all their names right, too.

SEBASTIAN

She did, by God.
(*He goes back to his table, stands and reads strip of information to himself.*)

ESSIE

The things we told them about themselves—that information cost
us plenty!
(*She goes back to her table.*)

SEBASTIAN

And believe me, Josef, when Essie pays money for anything, it's
important.

JOSEF

It's important for me to stay out of jail.

ESSIE

(*Sitting*)

Joey, you take these things too seriously. You'll make yourself ill.

SEBASTIAN

(*Going to* ESSIE)

Don't waste any sympathy on Josef—we could have made General Zandek's hair stand on end with this stuff. (*Referring to the strip of paper*) "Born in Ostrava—November 7, 1910. Lost in the forest for forty-eight hours when he was five years old"—you know he'd never imagine we'd know a thing like that!—"At nineteen he broke his leg mountain-climbing—at military school, he was very unpopular."

JOSEF

And you would have told him that?

ESSIE

Yes.

SEBASTIAN

"At sixteen he got the mayor's daughter in trouble. Her name was Bozena Trnkova."

ESSIE

What was that name?

SEBASTIAN

"Bozena Trnkova . . . ."

ESSIE

Bozena Trnkova? . . . That's trouble enough for any girl.

SEBASTIAN

And the poor town clerk had to marry her.

ESSIE

At least she got a new name out of it.
(*Taking their pay envelope from her pocket, she begins to count their money.*)

SEBASTIAN

(*Continuing*)
"Very sentimental about his mother! She died when he was very young. Her pet name for him was Pepi." Essie—his mother's pet name for him was Pepi! Oh, God, what we could have done with that. Josef, remember—wherever a man's mother is concerned, he's a complete pushover. I'll never forgive you for not telling us General Zandek was out front.
(*He goes back to his own table and sits.*)

JOSEF

I'd rather you never forgive me than me never forgive me.
(ESSIE *has finished her counting.*)

ESSIE

Here—what's this?

JOSEF

What's what?

ESSIE

There's a lot missing! You've docked our salary!

JOSEF

(*Going to* ESSIE)
Madame, every week I have explained. (*Pointing to figures on the envelope*) I've got it all written out, see? This is the state tax, this is the city tax—and because this is your last week in the country they've deducted the tax on foreign acts—two thousand crowns.

SEBASTIAN

Foreign act! I'm a Czech citizen! I was born in this country.

JOSEF

But your wife wasn't.

SEBASTIAN

Then tax her.

ESSIE

Yes. Give me back his thousand crowns.

JOSEF

I'm sorry, but you have been declared a foreign act.

SEBASTIAN

How can they declare us a—

JOSEF
(*Interrupting*)
Don't blame me! These decisions are in the hands of the Cultural Action Committee.

ESSIE

Is that that little snip who comes around here every week begging for money?

JOSEF

Madame, they do not beg. Contributions to the Cultural Action Committee are voluntary—twenty-five per cent of your salary.

ESSIE

We're not volunteering.

JOSEF

Madame, when you have no chance of winning an argument, it's best not to argue. (*There is a knock on the sitting-room door*) I'll see who it is.
(*He crosses through the sitting room.*)

THE GREAT SEBASTIANS

SEBASTIAN
(*Taking off his trousers*)
If that's the man to take our trunks to the station, tell him they're not ready yet.
(JOSEF *opens the door, and* MANYA *is standing there.*)

JOSEF
It's Manya. Are you free to see Manya?
(MANYA *strides into the sitting room.*)

ESSIE
(*Rising, crossing to the sitting room*)
Manya? Who's Manya? (MANYA *has stopped in front of the table. As she sees* MANYA) Oh. It's you.

JOSEF
Manya's our hard-working little representative of the Cultural Action Committee.

SEBASTIAN
(*Crossing to the sitting room with his trousers in his hands*)
Is it you we have to thank for being taxed as a foreign act? I, who was born and nearly finished high school in Czechoslovakia?

MANYA
These decisions are made by the Central Committee, Mr. Sebastian.

ESSIE
Let me tell you something, miss. We have a bit of influence here. We have an old friend in the government.

SEBASTIAN
We had lunch with him today.

ESSIE
We'll ask him.

MANYA

There is no appeal from decisions made by the Central Committee, Madame. And you've got me into trouble at headquarters!

SEBASTIAN

Well, that makes us even, doesn't it!
(He goes back into the dressing room and puts his trousers on a trunk hanger.)

MANYA
(Following him to the center door)
You are the only act that's played this theatre that hasn't given the full voluntary assessment. However, since this is your last night and you can't take Czechoslovakian money out of the country, a substantial contribution will make the Central Committee pleased with all of us.

ESSIE

You can tell the Central Committee they can bloody well—

SEBASTIAN

Essie! Now, you let me handle this.

ESSIE
(Crosses to her dressing table)
You can handle it, but you're not going to give them one heller! *(She sits.)*

MANYA

Mr. Sebastian, as a citizen of Czechoslovakia, I'm sure that—

SEBASTIAN
(Interrupting)
One moment, please! *(He strides back into the sitting room, pantless, takes* MANYA *by the elbow and conducts her toward the door, down right, as he speaks)* In the eyes of the Central Committee I am not a citizen of Czechoslovakia. I am a foreign act. Very well. I accept their ruling. And as of this moment, nothing would be more foreign to my act than to give money to your committee!

34

MANYA

(*Breaking away from his hold*)

Mr. Sebastian, you'd better understand! In this matter I represent the government of Czechoslovakia!

SEBASTIAN

A fine government you represent; Trying to chisel us out of twenty-five per cent of our salary. Even our agent, the dirty crook, only gets ten!

MANYA

I shall report what you've said!
(*She turns and exits.*)

SEBASTIAN

(*Following her out into the hall*)

And be sure you quote me correctly!

JOSEF

There's a train at seven in the morning.

SEBASTIAN

(*Re-entering*)

We're booked on it.

JOSEF

Please catch it before the nick of time.
(SEBASTIAN *crosses into the dressing room.*)

ESSIE

Rudi, you were marvelous!

SEBASTIAN

Yes, wasn't I?
(*He goes into the alcove.*)

35

JOSEF

I hope you'll have no trouble at the border, I'm afraid. Have your papers in order. (*Going to* ESSIE) Have your money counted. And good luck, I hope.
(*He kisses* ESSIE's *hand.*)

ESSIE

Good-bye, Joey.
(*Sebastian comes out of the alcove in his dressing gown.*)

JOSEF

Oh, I forgot. You haven't signed for your salary.
(*Takes salary list from his pocket.*)

ESSIE

We didn't get our full salary. I'm not sure I should sign my full name.

JOSEF

You'd better. I have to turn this in to the government now. (*His eyes light on an envelope on Sebastian's dressing table, and he points to it*) Have you any special interest in postage stamps?
(ESSIE *turns quickly, looks at* JOSEF.)

ESSIE
(*Sharply*)

Why do you ask that?

JOSEF

My little boy saves stamps. (*He picks up the envelope*) I was just going to ask could I give him the stamp from that letter. It's an English stamp.

SEBASTIAN

Well, why not? (*He takes the envelope, removes the contents*) From our son to your son. This is a letter from our boy Christopher.

36

JOSEF

You have a son?
(SEBASTIAN *picks up a framed picture from* ESSIE'S *table.*)

SEBASTIAN

Yes, and a daughter, too.
(*He shows the picture to* JOSEF.)

ESSIE

Yes, Edie. She's being married next Tuesday. We're giving her all her house linen for a wedding present.

SEBASTIAN

Her young man's father owns a bank.

JOSEF

You must be very happy.

ESSIE

Well, in a way, yes. But she's marrying outside the profession.

JOSEF

And your boy? How old is he?

ESSIE

Sixteen. He's still at school.

SEBASTIAN

Jan Masaryk is his godfather. You'll hear from him—in the legit. You should have seen him last year in his school play as Lady Macbeth.

ESSIE

Oh, he was beautiful. We'll all be together for the Easter holidays . . . the whole family, the first time in five years. Whooo! . . .
(*She spins a complete circle on her stool.*)

JOSEF

That's fine.

ESSIE

We don't get together very often, you know—traveling.

JOSEF

Well, I'll tell my boy the stamp came from the Great Sebastians.

SEBASTIAN

Does your boy save autographs, too?

JOSEF

No.

SEBASTIAN

Well, he does now. He can begin with mine.
(*He autographs the envelope and hands it to* JOSEF.)

JOSEF

Thank you— (*Starting for door down right*) —and good luck. Oh,
I said that before. Well—who can tell?
(JOSEF *exits, down right.*)

ESSIE

(*Rising and taking her hatbox to the hamper*)
Joey has changed. He used to be such a happy man.

SEBASTIAN

Was there any reason you didn't want him to have that postage
stamp?

ESSIE

No. Why?

SEBASTIAN

You acted as though you didn't like his asking for it.

38

ESSIE

(*Putting the hatbox in the hamper*)
No, but it did give me a bit of a turn.

SEBASTIAN

What did?

ESSIE

Never mind. I'll tell you later.

SEBASTIAN

(*The moralist*)
Essie, whenever you don't want to tell me what you're doing, you're doing something you should tell me what you're doing. Are you smuggling again?

ESSIE

That depends on how you look at it.

SEBASTIAN

Essie, I don't want to be held up all day at the border tomorrow while they search us.

ESSIE

Let them search. They'll never find this.

SEBASTIAN

Find what?

ESSIE

Never mind.
(*She slams down the lid of the hamper and straightens up.*)

SEBASTIAN

Essie! You must tell me! You know how I feel. I've always tried to be an honest man.

ESSIE

The less you know, the more honest you can feel.
(*She crosses back to her table and putters around with articles on it.*)

SEBASTIAN

Essie, please tell me! I not only want to feel honest, but I want to feel sure you can get away with it.

ESSIE

Now look, Rudi. We've earned quite a bit of money here, and it all belongs to us. You don't think I'm going to leave it here, do you?

SEBASTIAN

If they search you and find any money—
(*He paces down left.*)

ESSIE

They won't find any money.

SEBASTIAN

Well, what will they find?

ESSIE

They won't find anything. And if you want to see it, look in my compact.
(*He takes her compact off the dressing table and looks into it.*)

SEBASTIAN

There's nothing in here.

ESSIE

Give it to me.
(*He does. She takes a nail file, scrapes carefully under the powder and comes up with a stamp. She blows the powder off and shows it to him.*)

SEBASTIAN

Just a postage stamp.

ESSIE

(*Proudly*)
There are only three others like it in the whole world!

SEBASTIAN

But Chris doesn't save postage stamps any more—

ESSIE

No, but I do. If we can save this stamp until we get to England, it'll be worth over a thousand pounds! What price Edie's wedding present, now?

SEBASTIAN

(*He takes the stamp from her*)
Well, I'll be damned! You know, Essie, we've been asked at more borders whether we've got tobacco, perfume, liquor, currency, but we've never been asked whether we have postage stamps! Oh, Essie, we won't have to lie about this at all! And I think you can get away with it.
(*There is a knock at the sitting-room door, down right.* SEBASTIAN *tries to hand the stamp back to her, but her attention is diverted.*)

ESSIE

(*Looking toward the door*)
There's someone at the door.

SEBASTIAN

Quickly!

ESSIE

(*Still looking toward the door*)
Key!

SEBASTIAN

Quickly!

ESSIE

Key!

SEBASTIAN

No, I mean hide it! Quickly! (ESSIE *takes the stamp, puts it back in the powder, closes the compact and puts it in her pocket. There is another knock on the door.* SEBASTIAN *crosses toward the outer door, down right. He gets to the door and looks back to make sure* ESSIE *has hidden the stamp*) Who is it?

JOSEF
(Off)

It's me—Josef!
(SEBASTIAN *opens the door.*)

SEBASTIAN

What is it?
(JOSEF *rushes past* SEBASTIAN *into the room nervously.*)

JOSEF

Close the door! (SEBASTIAN *does so*) I was afraid this would happen and it's going to!

ESSIE

Josef, if you're determined to have a nervous breakdown, don't have it in our dressing room!

JOSEF

General Zandek is coming backstage. He has asked to see you!

SEBASTIAN

Essie! General Zandek liked the act.
(ESSIE *goes into the sitting room.*)

JOSEF

Please—do me this one favor. Those things you know about Zandek—do not use them in my theatre. Wait till you get to his home.

SEBASTIAN

His home?

JOSEF

Yes. Every Saturday night he gives a late supper party. He will ask you to be there.

ESSIE

What makes you think so?

JOSEF

He always asks one or two acts to entertain his guests.

ESSIE

Oh—does he pay well?

JOSEF

He doesn't pay at all.

ESSIE

Then to hell with him! We never entertain for nothing. Don't you know the record of the Great Sebastians? We've never played a benefit.
(*She crosses back into the dressing room and sits.*)

JOSEF

But you can't refuse General Zandek—he may be the next Minister of Defense!

SEBASTIAN

(*Unimpressed, he waves* JOSEF *off and crosses into the dressing room*)
Huh-huh-huh-huh! . . .

JOSEF
(*Following him*)
Please! . . . You've got to go—it's like a command performance!

SEBASTIAN
Let him command Fink's Mules.

JOSEF
Sebastian, if he asks you to go, you have to go.

SEBASTIAN
Josef, General Zandek can't make us go to his house, and you know he can't.

JOSEF
No. He can't make you go, but he can make you wish you had.

ESSIE
No pay, no go. Tell him we're busy.

JOSEF
Only the fact that you are sick would be considered an excuse.

ESSIE
The thought of working for nothing always makes me sick.

JOSEF
Before I bring him here, I'll present Libusa—you know, the juggler. (*He describes the handwork of a juggler with gestures, and starts for the door, down right*) Perhaps he'll choose her, or maybe the Havlicek Sisters. Let's hope he didn't like you.
(*He exits, down right, much agitated.*)

44

ESSIE

(*Rises*)

We can't refuse to meet him. I'd better go put on something decent. (*She goes to the alcove entrance*) Rudi, he may not understand artists. Put on your trousers.

(ESSIE *exits into alcove.*)

SEBASTIAN

(*He gets his trousers from a hook on the back wall and puts them on*)

It's a damn shame, Essie. All that information. Date of his birth—lost in the forest—breaking his leg mountain-climbing—and the mayor's daughter! Whooo! . . . We could have made his eyes pop out of his head with that stuff.

(*He picks up the strip of paper with the Zandek information and puts it in his dressing-gown pocket.*)

ESSIE

(*Off*)

Yes, and wind up giving another half-hour show for nothing.

SEBASTIAN

Well, it's very hard to resist reading a person's mind when you know what's in his mind.

ESSIE

(*Off*)

Now Rudi, please don't try to impress him. I'm not sure we should even try to be attractive. (*She comes out of the alcove in a stunning negligee, looking very attractive*) We've got to pack here, we've got to pack at the hotel, we've got a train to catch—and besides all that, and don't you forget it, I'm ill.

(*There is a knock at the door.* ESSIE *is rouging her cheeks at her dressing table.*)

SEBASTIAN

Then stop making yourself look so healthy. (*He crosses toward the door, down right. He opens the door and* SERGEANT JAVORSKY *enters and crosses toward the dressing room.* SEBASTIAN *is obviously disappointed*) Take your time, Essie, it's only a Sergeant.

SERGEANT JAVORSKY

You are about to be honored by a visit from **General Zandek.**
(*The* SERGEANT *looks about the room, strolls into the dressing room, looks into the alcove.* ESSIE *and* SEBASTIAN *watch this with some surprise, and when the* SERGEANT *peers into the alcove,* ESSIE *gestures a swat at his backside with her hair brush.*)

SEBASTIAN

We've got nothing up our sleeves.

SERGEANT JAVORSKY
(*Smiles at this, turns and crosses into the sitting room*)
The General can be much more pleasant when he feels safe.
(SERGEANT JAVORSKY *exits down right.*)

ESSIE

Who does he think we are—Jack the Ripper?

SERGEANT JAVORSKY
(*Off*)
Everything in order, sir.
(*After a second,* JOSEF *enters followed by* GENERAL ZANDEK, *who is carrying his hat and gloves.*)

JOSEF

General Zandek, the Great Sebastian—General Otokar Zandek.
(ZANDEK *and* SEBASTIAN *bow.* JOSEF *exits.*)

SEBASTIAN

General Zandek, you do us a great honor.

ZANDEK
(*Taking* SEBASTIAN'S *hand*)
It's a pleasure. I knew your voice very well during the war.

46

SEBASTIAN

Oh, my broadcasts.

ZANDEK

Yes. Your broadcasts were a great help to us of the resistance movement.

SEBASTIAN

You make me very happy.

ZANDEK

I came backstage to thank you.

SEBASTIAN

You are very kind.

ZANDEK

And for your performance tonight.

SEBASTIAN

Oh, you enjoyed it?

ZANDEK

It was very entertaining.

SEBASTIAN

Thank you. Thank you. My wife will want to hear that. (*Goes to center door*) Madame? Madame— (*During the above introduction,* ESSIE *has tucked her salary in her stocking and is now tucking a rose in her bosom. She enters the sitting room*) May I present General Zandek. My wife, Madame Sebastian.

ZANDEK

Madame!
 (*He kisses her hand.*)

47

ESSIE

How do you do, General? (*She sits, left of table*) Oh! Forgive me,
I must sit down. I'm not very well tonight.
    (ZANDEK *sits, right of table*.)

SEBASTIAN
(Above the table)
The performance is so exhausting for her.

ESSIE

I tried so hard tonight—I felt the presence of someone in the audience—someone with a powerful mind.

SEBASTIAN

It must have been you, General.

ZANDEK

I suppose my mind was too powerful for you to read.

SEBASTIAN

Oh, not too—not too. We wouldn't want to embarrass you by making you part of our entertainment. (*To* ESSIE) The General said he
enjoyed the act very much.

ESSIE

Oh, that's ever so nice.

ZANDEK

I was here Tuesday, Wednesday and Thursday night, too. I
dropped in just to see your performance.

ESSIE

And here again tonight. You pay us a great compliment.

ZANDEK

No—I was looking for something.

ESSIE

Oh?

ZANDEK

I've always thought that the reading of minds—genuine mind reading—could be of service to someone—let us say—in my position.

ESSIE

That's very interesting.

SEBASTIAN

Yes, that's a very exciting thought.

ZANDEK

Yes, I was excited myself—until tonight.

ESSIE

Tonight?

SEBASTIAN

Until tonight?

ZANDEK

Watching you tonight I realized everything I saw was a trick. I
couldn't always explain it—a signal—a confederate—

SEBASTIAN

And you came backstage to tell us that?

ZANDEK

Oh, I admire your ability to entertain.

ESSIE

Well, thank you.

49

ZANDEK

And I am sure the audience was convinced you were genuine.
(SEBASTIAN *gives a cigarette to* ESSIE *and the* GENERAL *and takes one for himself.*)

SEBASTIAN

But you were not.

ZANDEK

Unhappily, no. You, sir, are a delightful faker and Madame a charming charlatan.

SEBASTIAN

Well, if that's what you really believe, General, we mustn't keep you any longer. You have been so kind—

ZANDEK

No, no, no, please—I have plenty of time. Tell me frankly. Do you claim that you actually can read minds?
(SEBASTIAN *lights* ZANDEK's *cigarette.*)

SEBASTIAN

Frankly, our reputation speaks for itself.
(SEBASTIAN *lights* ESSIE's *cigarette.*)

ZANDEK

I am a military scientist. I must have evidence. I deal only with proven facts. (SEBASTIAN *prepares to light his own cigarette, but* ZANDEK *reaches up and pulls his arm down, blowing out the match*) Please—not three on a match!
(ESSIE *and* SEBASTIAN *exchange a look.*)

ESSIE

Rudi, does it occur to you that General Zandek could be taken for your Uncle Michael?

SEBASTIAN

Yes—I think he could be taken! (*To* ZANDEK) So you must have evidence, General? Place in your mind the date of your birth. Concentrate.

ZANDEK

Good.
(He closes his eyes.)

SEBASTIAN
(In the act now)
Madame, would you care to . . . ?

ESSIE
(In her trance of concentration)
November . . .

SEBASTIAN

And the date . . . ?
(He realizes he doesn't remember the date. He and ESSIE *exchange looks; He moves behind* ZANDEK, *quickly gets out the yellow strip of paper from his pocket, consults the information on it.)*

ESSIE

Oh, General, you have got a powerful mind. I see numbers exploding like fireworks—

SEBASTIAN
(Crosses down right behind ZANDEK, *looks at* ESSIE)
And the date? . . .
(SEBASTIAN *smooths down his hair with his right hand.)*

ESSIE
(As SEBASTIAN *gives her this cue for the number seven)*
November—the seventh—

51

SEBASTIAN

(Giving her another sight cue: right forefinger on cheek,
indicating ten)

And the year? . . .

ESSIE

Nineteen hundred . . . and ten. November the seventh, 1910.

SEBASTIAN

Is that correct?

ZANDEK

(Turning to SEBASTIAN*)*

Very good. But I am a national hero. The date of my birth is
known to everyone in Czechoslovakia. I am afraid that includes
Madame Sebastian.

SEBASTIAN

General, I can assure you that Madame Sebastian did not know
the date of your birth. However, General—there are things about
you that we do know. For instance, we know that you have the reputation of being irresistible to women.

ZANDEK

I have? That will give me new confidence.

ESSIE

There is one woman who has been in your thoughts for many
years.

ZANDEK

Yes—which one?

ESSIE

You had trouble with her father.

ZANDEK

That could be one of several.

ESSIE

I read her name—Bozena—

ZANDEK

(*Trying to place her*)

Bozena?

ESSIE

(*None too sure she remembers it*)

Bozena . . . Trnkova.

ZANDEK

(*Recalling*)

Oh! . . . the little daughter of the mayor! You do astonish me!

ESSIE

Now do you think I'm a charming charlatan?

ZANDEK

Charming, yes—and still a charlatan. She was not in my thoughts. As a matter of fact, I haven't thought of her for years. Her name was not in my mind.

SEBASTIAN

(*Crossing upstage to above table*)

Not in your conscious mind—but in your subconscious mind.

ESSIE

She has never been out of your subconscious mind.

SEBASTIAN

General, there are many people who can read the conscious mind. But what makes the Great Sebastians unique is that they can read the subconscious mind.

ESSIE

Things that happen when you are very young lie buried in the subconscious for many years.

SEBASTIAN

Early triumphs—early fears—
(*He casts a prompting glance down at* ESSIE.)

ESSIE

You—had a painful experience when you were—about nineteen. I see you being carried down a mountainside—Oh! . . . You broke your leg climbing a mountain.

ZANDEK
(*A little disturbed*)

That is true. . . . That is true! How did you ever— (*He becomes more practical*) What mountain?

ESSIE

(*Completely unprepared; shooting a quick glance at* SEBASTIAN, *then pretending to concentrate again*)

It's a very large mountain—there are trees—(*Glancing again at* SEBASTIAN) There is snow on the peak—I think!

ZANDEK

Yes, but the name. (*Closing his eyes, fiercely concentrating*) I am thinking of the name. Read from my mind the name!
(ESSIE *hesitates.* SEBASTIAN *comes to her rescue.*)

SEBASTIAN
(*Crossing down left of* ESSIE)

General, we cannot work in a hostile atmosphere. The channel from your mind to Madame's must be opened by a willingness to believe.

ZANDEK

I am willing to believe! I wanted to be convinced! (*He rises*) I am disappointed not to be convinced. Now I will go. (*He gives a sigh of disappointment, then goes to the door, down right. He opens the door and calls off*) Sergeant! (*He turns back to the* SEBASTIANS *and, picking up his hat and gloves*) I had hoped you could be of use to me. You are clever, but you are fakes.

54

ESSIE

You have your opinion of us—and we have our opinion of you.
(*The* SERGEANT *comes through the door and stands at attention.*)

ZANDEK

(*To the* SERGEANT)

Bring my car around to the stage door. (ZANDEK *turns as if to ad-
dress a last remark to the* SEBASTIANS, *then looks back at the* SERGEANT,
who hasn't moved. He speaks angrily) Quickly!

ESSIE

(*Automatically*)

Key!
(ZANDEK *looks at* ESSIE, *looks back at the* SERGEANT.)

ZANDEK

What are you waiting for?

SERGEANT JAVORSKY

I'm waiting for the key, sir.
(ZANDEK *stares in amazement at* ESSIE. *Without taking his eyes
from her, he reaches into his pocket, gets his car key and extends it to* SERGEANT JAVORSKY *who takes it and exits.*)

ZANDEK

(*To* ESSIE)

You read his mind!

SEBASTIAN

(*Coming downstage with a broad gesture of the hand*)
He was not hostile.

ZANDEK

Perhaps you can help me after all. Perhaps there is a chance; it's
worth taking. We shall see. I am having some guests at my house for
supper tonight. You will be there at twelve o'clock.
(*He puts on his hat.*)

SEBASTIAN

We appreciate the honor, but . . .

ZANDEK

You will be there!

ESSIE

Sorry, General, you will forgive us—

ZANDEK

There is something I need to know. You will help me find out. At my house—twelve o'clock!
(*With this order, he turns and exits.* SEBASTIAN *slams the door shut behind* ZANDEK *and turns to* ESSIE.)

ESSIE

I told you not to try to impress him.

SEBASTIAN

Who impressed him! You impressed him! You remembered a cue and at the wrong time. You even impressed me!

ESSIE

Rudi—don't joke. I don't like it. I don't like it a bit.

SEBASTIAN

Neither do I.

ESSIE

He wants to use us for something.

SEBASTIAN

I know. I wish I knew what for.

ESSIE

What are we going to do when we get there?

SEBASTIAN

Well, the written message bit is always good. But remember—we'll be in a house, not a theatre.

ESSIE

What'll I wear?

SEBASTIAN

Now's your chance to wear that dress.

ESSIE

Oh, yes.

SEBASTIAN

Oh, God!

(*He starts into the dressing room.*)

ESSIE

What?

SEBASTIAN

(*Crossing down left*)

This is the first time we've used the new code in a house.

ESSIE

(*Following him into the dressing room*)

Oh, Rudi!

SEBASTIAN

(*Turning to her, giving her a word signal*)

Madame, would you be good enough to—

ESSIE

Book.

57

SEBASTIAN

Madame, can you identify—

ESSIE

Ash tray.

SEBASTIAN

Madame, can you get the impression of—

ESSIE

Cigarette box. (*She crosses to her dressing table*) We've got all that packing to do at the hotel, too. Oh, I do hate these private parties. They always give you something with a long number on it.

SEBASTIAN

Yes, and you need work on numbers. Essie, watch.
(*He begins to give her sight cues.*)

ESSIE

(*As he pretends to adjust his necktie*) Nine . . . (*As he touches handkerchief in his breast pocket*) Three . . . (*As he smooths his hair with his right hand*) Six—er—seven!

SEBASTIAN

What's the matter with you?

ESSIE

I've got one of my feelings—one of my creepy feelings. (*As he slaps his hands together*) Five. It always means trouble. (*He smooths his hair again*) Seven. We won't get any sleep tonight at all.
(*She sits at her table, facing* SEBASTIAN.)

SEBASTIAN

(*Pacing*)

I know. But that's not what worries me. What I want to know is what's that General up to?

ESSIE

I haven't the faintest idea.

SEBASTIAN

He says he wants us to find out something.

ESSIE

I know. I heard him.
(SEBASTIAN *sits at his dressing table.*)

SEBASTIAN

Essie—Essie, what do you suppose it is? What do you suppose he wants us to find out?

ESSIE

How should I know? What do you think I am, a mind reader?
(SEBASTIAN *continues his sight cues as*

The Curtain Falls

ACT TWO

ACT TWO

The living room of GENERAL ZANDEK'S *villa on the outskirts of Prague.*

The room is furnished in continental style. The walls of the room are covered in dark green brocaded velvet. The woodwork and doors are painted in a green similar to the walls, though somewhat lighter, and trimmed in gold. The pilasters and cornice are in burnished gold. The room is carpeted in taupe, sculptured carpeting.

There is a rounded arch, up center, with sliding doors. We can see in the hallway a flight of stairs leading to the upper floor. These stairs start with a curve and disappear up and off right. The front door of the house is off the hallway, left. The dining room and kitchen are off the hallway, right. In the lower half of the right wall of the room there is a French window. Inside this window there is an iron grille which is bolted. The grille opens into the room. The windows open off. Above the windows the right wall slants to meet the back wall just right of the arch. The opposite side of the room is similar in shape. In the diagonal wall left of the arch is a door to an anteroom, up two steps. In the lower left wall there is an arched, windowed alcove large enough to house a baby grand piano and stool.

A small crystal chandelier hangs in the center of the hall. There are matching crystal sconces on either side of the arch, in the living room.

There is a velvet appliquéd throw draped over the piano, on which rest a lamp, a bowl of low white flowers and a stemmed white china bowl. On the upstage wall of the alcove hangs a dark Renaissance painting in a heavy gold frame.

On stage of the incurve of the piano there is a little single-seated loveseat. Directly right of it is a small round gilt table. Onstage of this is a Louis XV straight chair. On the table sits a miniature red Chinese lacquered chest of drawers.

On either side of the arch against the upstage back wall, there is a Louis XV straight chair.

Against the right stage diagonal, between the arch and the grilled French windows, is a red Chinese lacquered antique cabinet.

THE GREAT SEBASTIANS

Down right center at an angle corresponding with the French doors is an ornate desk. On the downstage right corner of the desk is a continental dial telephone, and centered on the onstage side is a glass inkwell-tray containing a pen. Above it is a brown leather cigarette box. At the desk is another chair, and left of the desk is a small straight chair.

In the hall, in the curve of the staircase, is a long bench with high, curved arms. On it, several men's coats and hats have been thrown.

AT RISE: *The stage is empty. We hear music coming from off right, mostly American jazz, played in two-step rhythm.* SERGEANT JAVORSKY *enters from up right of arch with two plates of food. He puts them down on the desk, then unbolts the grille, down right. He opens it and the windows and calls off.* . . . .

SERGEANT JAVORSKY

Salda! Novak!
 (*He goes back of the desk, takes a cigarette from the box and lights it. The* FIRST *and* SECOND SOLDIERS *enter through the French windows and come to attention.*)

FIRST SOLDIER

Yes, Sergeant.

SERGEANT JAVORSKY
 (*Indicating food*)
I brought you something from the kitchen.

SECOND SOLDIER

Us?
 (*They move in and pick up the plates.*)

SERGEANT JAVORSKY

Why not? The General does very well by himself and his friends.
 (FIRST SOLDIER *looks at his plate and shows it to the* SECOND SOLDIER.)

FIRST SOLDIER

Look, Salda! (*To the* SERGEANT) Where did you ever get food like this?

64

SERGEANT JAVORSKY

That's what they're eating.
(*The* SOLDIERS *start to eat rapidly.*)

FIRST SOLDIER

Who's in there—some big brass?

SERGEANT JAVORSKY

Yes, and some big brassières.

FIRST SOLDIER

You know, the Sergeant that was here before you. . . .

SECOND SOLDIER

He wouldn't even tell us what they had for dinner!

SERGEANT JAVORSKY

Your job is to guard the General. You should have some good reason for keeping him alive.

SECOND SOLDIER

This is the first good reason I've seen.

SERGEANT JAVORSKY

You men have no kick coming. This is a lot easier than border duty.

FIRST SOLDIER

But not as much fun. My brother's on border duty. Once in a while he gets a chance to shoot at somebody.

SERGEANT JAVORSKY

(*Sitting at the desk*)
I suppose the General himself tips you off when he's expecting someone to slip through the river-road gate.
(*The offstage music stops.*)

FIRST SOLDIER

Nobody comes through there.

SERGEANT JAVORSKY

Not even one of his girls now and then?

SECOND SOLDIER

If any girls come into this house, they come through the front door.

FIRST SOLDIER

We're not there to let people come through—we're there to see that they don't.

SERGEANT JAVORSKY

I see. The General's a little nervous, isn't he? Well, today everybody is. (*The doorbell rings. They look toward the front door, nervously alert*) Outside! Quick! Here—take this. (SERGEANT JAVORSKY *hands his lighted cigarette to the* FIRST SOLDIER) Close the windows!
(*The* SOLDIERS *go out, closing the windows behind them. The* SERGEANT *closes the grille, bolting it. He picks up the two plates on desk, and hurries off, up right, re-enters quickly, dusting his hands off, and hurriedly crosses through the hall and off left.*)

SERGEANT JAVORSKY
(*Off*)

Good evening!

SEBASTIAN
(*Off*)

Good evening. The Great Sebastians.

SERGEANT JAVORSKY
(*Off*)

Certainly. This way, please.
(*He crosses back into the room and stands at attention, right of the arch.* SEBASTIAN *and* ESSIE *sweep into the hall and into the room, in a terrific entrance. They are both in evening*

dress. They are wearing long black velvet capes, lined with cloth of gold. On the front of each is a gold-embroidered letter "s" in a sunburst. They are both chagrined to find that the room is empty and that a good entrance has been wasted.)

SEBASTIAN

(Gliding quickly from embarrassment to aplomb)
I was afraid we were late. (*He consults his watch*) The General said midnight.

ESSIE

I told you nobody that's anybody gets to a party on time.

SEBASTIAN

(Concerned)
I'm sorry I rushed you, Essie.

ESSIE

(Aggrieved)
We're the first ones here.

SEBASTIAN

I apologize, Essie.

ESSIE

People might think we were hungry.

SERGEANT JAVORSKY

May I take your cape, Madame?
(*He removes the cape from her shoulders, throws it over his arm.*)

ESSIE

You're always early. I've spent half my married life waiting with you in railway stations.

SEBASTIAN

I said I'm sorry.

SERGEANT JAVORSKY

Your cape, sir?
(SEBASTIAN *slips out of it with the* SERGEANT'S *help; the* SERGEANT *throws it over his arm and starts for the anteroom.*)

ESSIE

(*Consulting mirror in her evening bag*)
Every time you rush me this way you ruin my make-up. Look at my hair. I'm a sight!
(*There isn't a hair out of place.*)

SERGEANT JAVORSKY

I'll put these in this anteroom. (*He starts up the steps*) Then I'll tell the General you are here. He and his guests are at supper.
(*He exits into the anteroom.*)

SEBASTIAN

Then we are late! I told you so, Essie, I told you so!

ESSIE

Never mind, Rudi. Never mind.

SEBASTIAN

The hours I've spent waiting for you—fixing your eyelashes—

ESSIE

That's enough.

SEBASTIAN

—Then running back to dab perfume behind your ears—tell me, has anyone ever sniffed behind your ears?

ESSIE

Rudi, don't be vulgar. Come on! Let's join the General.
(*She makes a start for the arch;* SEBASTIAN *stops her.*)

SEBASTIAN

Essie, we have to wait for that soldier to announce us.
(*From off right the music starts again.*)

ESSIE

I'm hungry, Rudi. I haven't eaten since lunch.

SEBASTIAN

Well, neither have I—but we've got to stay hungry for a couple of minutes. We've got to pump this fellow while we have a chance. We've got to find out something about the other guests. How can we read their minds if we don't know anything about them? Besides— we don't even know how many there are.

ESSIE

We only need a little on one or two of them. We're not going to give them more than ten minutes. (*Looking around the room*) There's something about this house I don't like. Oh, I wish we hadn't got into this.

SEBASTIAN

Don't worry—we'll get a good supper out of it, anyway.
(*The* SERGEANT *enters from the anteroom.*)

SERGEANT JAVORSKY

Just make yourselves comfortable.
(*He crosses in front of them and starts out the arch.*)

SEBASTIAN

I beg your pardon?
(*The* SERGEANT *stops.*)

SERGEANT JAVORSKY

You are to wait here until the General and his guests have finished supper.

ESSIE

But we're the General's guests. We were invited to supper.

SERGEANT JAVORSKY

No, Madame. You are the General's entertainers. You were invited to entertain.

ESSIE

Rudi, did you hear that?

SEBASTIAN

There must be some mistake!

SERGEANT JAVORSKY

The General has entertainers here every Saturday night. They are never allowed to sit at the General's table.
(*He starts off.*)

SEBASTIAN

Hah—We're good enough to sit at table with Mr. Masaryk—

SERGEANT JAVORSKY

Masaryk—?

ESSIE

But not good enough for that potty old General!

SERGEANT JAVORSKY

You know Jan Masaryk?

SEBASTIAN

Yes. We happen to be old friends. We had lunch with him today.

SERGEANT JAVORSKY

You did, sir?

SEBASTIAN

Yes. Does that surprise you? Now perhaps you'll tell the General we'll have supper with him?

SERGEANT JAVORSKY

Yes, sir.

ESSIE

And if he starts to argue, tell him the Great Sebastians never read minds on an empty stomach.

(SERGEANT JAVORSKY *exits. The* SEBASTIANS *quickly begin to "case" the room:* SEBASTIAN *crosses to the desk, begins to look through the drawers, while* ESSIE *searches the Chinese antique cabinet.*)

ESSIE

He's bloody neat!

SEBASTIAN

He's bloody careful. Not a damn thing.

ESSIE

Never mind. We still have all that information on him we haven't used yet.

SEBASTIAN

Yes—lost in the forest—what was it his mother called him?

ESSIE

Pepi.

SEBASTIAN

Very unpopular at military academy.

ESSIE

Don't you forget that. One peep out of Pepi and we'll use it.
(*Their eyes have been searching the room for useful information.* SEBASTIAN *goes to the anteroom door.*)

SEBASTIAN

(*Indicating the hallway*)

Essie, stand there.
(*He goes into the anteroom as* ESSIE *goes to the left of the arch
and watches off right.*)

ESSIE

Stay up all night, give him a free show—get insulted the minute
you come in the door!

SEBASTIAN

(*Returning from the anteroom*)

Nothing but evening wraps. No clues—no handbags.

ESSIE

(*Pointing to coats on the bench in the hallway*)

Rudi, look. Gentlemen's coats. (*Going downstage left to search a
miniature chest of drawers on the table*) Expects us to work without
food—without information—the old poop! (*She looks in each little
drawer*) Cleaned out his desk just to be nasty. He's got a suspicious
mind, he has. Not open and aboveboard as people should be.
(*The offstage music has stopped.* SEBASTIAN *has found a letter
in a coat pocket.*)

SEBASTIAN

(*Coming into the arch*)

Psst! Essie! (*Reading the envelope*) Mr. and Mrs. Karel Cerny.
C-E-R-N-Y.

ESSIE

Cerny—Cerny. Know anything about him?

SEBASTIAN

(*Taking the letter out*)

No, but I will in a minute. His picture's been in the paper a lot. He's short; wears glasses with a ribbon.

ESSIE

Glasses with a ribbon.

SEBASTIAN

(*He has opened the letter and is reading it*)

This is from his mother. She lives in Bratislava.

ESSIE

Bratislava.

SEBASTIAN

Somebody's sick.

ESSIE

Good!

SEBASTIAN

In hospital.

ESSIE

That's enough on him. (SEBASTIAN *returns the letter to the coat and searches for another.* ESSIE *mutters*) Cerny. Hospital. Bratislava. Glasses with a ribbon.

SEBASTIAN

(*Having found another envelope*)

Novotny. Zikmund Novotny. I've seen his name, too. He's something high up—something in the Interior.

ESSIE

Interior of what?

SEBASTIAN

Interior of the government. . . They have something they call Interior. (*Looking at what he has removed from the envelope*) Oh, it's only a dentist bill. (*He returns the envelope to the coat.*)

ESSIE

What's the name of the man with the dentist's bill?

SEBASTIAN

Novotny. Zikmund Novotny.

ESSIE

Novotny. N-O-V-O-T-N-Y. Cerny. C-E-R-N-Y. Rudi, let's run what we've got.

SEBASTIAN

(*Circling down to her left, bending his knees to make himself "short"*) I wear glasses with a ribbon, and I'm short.

ESSIE
(*Extending her hand*)

Mr. Cerny—is it not?

SEBASTIAN
(*Takes her hand*)

Why yes, it is!

ESSIE

Why do I feel sympathy for you? I have an impression of worry— (*She stops acting*) Cerny. Hospital. Bratislava. Glasses with a ribbon. (*She gives up*) I'm hungry, Rudi. My brain won't work.

SEBASTIAN
(*He straightens up*)

All right. But now remember—when you get up from supper, you follow the ladies to the powder room. I don't know why it is, but people always talk more freely when they're near plumbing.
(*The* SERGEANT *enters with a tray on which are two plates of food and silverware, rolled in napkins.*)

74

SEBASTIAN

What's that?

SERGEANT JAVORSKY

The General says you were not invited to supper.

SEBASTIAN

Then we leave.
            (*He starts for the anteroom.*)

SERGEANT JAVORSKY

But I sneaked this food out of the kitchen for you!

SEBASTIAN

            (*As he goes into anteroom*)
Sneak it right back to the kitchen.

ESSIE

Another insult! Scraps from the kitchen!
            (*The* SERGEANT *holds the tray out for her to see.*)

SEBASTIAN

            (*Off*)
Rather than eat that, I'd starve.

ESSIE

            (*Staring at the food*)
Rudi! . . . Caviar! . . .

SEBASTIAN

            (*Re-entering*)
Caviar?
            (*He moves toward the tray.*)

ESSIE

And goose, I think.

SEBASTIAN

Goose?
> (*The offstage music starts again.*)

SERGEANT JAVORSKY

(*As he starts to back toward the desk, with the* SEBASTIANS *following*)
Yes, goose!
> (*The* SERGEANT *reaches the desk and puts the tray down. The*
> SEBASTIANS *pull up chairs and sit.*)

ESSIE

This is very cosy.
> (SEBASTIAN *removes the plates and napkins from the tray.*)

SERGEANT JAVORSKY
> (*Standing between them*)

Yes, Madame! You can depend on the army to have the best food—
and you can depend on General Zandek to have the best food in the
army!

SEBASTIAN

As a matter of fact, we prefer eating in private.

ESSIE

> (*Unfolding her napkin, tucking it in her bosom*)
Lovely goose! (*To the* SERGEANT) I'm very partial to a bit of goose.

SERGEANT JAVORSKY

Oh, the top people live off the top of the larder. (*Crossing to close
the anteroom door*) You've done very well today—(*Crosses back to
center*) —supper here, and lunch with Masaryk. So you really know
him!

SEBASTIAN

Oh, yes. Intimately. (*He takes a bite of food*) Old friends.

ESSIE

Rudi worked with him during the war, in London. (*She is looking at* SEBASTIAN's *plate*) Is that paté you've got? I haven't got any paté. (*She reaches over and scoops a forkful off his plate.*)

SEBASTIAN

(*Trying to ward her off*)

Well, leave me some.

ESSIE

I only took half. Fair's fair.

SERGEANT JAVORSKY

Did you know Masaryk in London, too, Madame?

SEBASTIAN

Did she know him! Mr. Masaryk used to say that my wife had more common sense than anybody in England. He loved talking to her.

ESSIE

(*Complacently*)

We got on very well.

SEBASTIAN

Many's the time he came to her for advice. (*Looking at her plate*) What kind of cheese is that?

ESSIE

Now, now, now—you eat off your own plate.

SEBASTIAN

You took most of my paté! (*He helps himself to her cheese*) Fair's fair, you said so yourself.

SERGEANT JAVORSKY

Well, Mr. Masaryk has plenty of problems now. (*Lightly*) What advice did you give him today? Did you tell him how to get an American loan?
(*They laugh.*)

77

ESSIE

He's a comic! Whoooo—this is fun!

SERGEANT JAVORSKY

I think you're having more fun in here than they are in there!

SEBASTIAN

Tell me, where are we supposed to give this entertainment—here in this room?

SERGEANT JAVORSKY

The entertainment is usually in here.

ESSIE

Then they must be comfortable—are there enough chairs? (*Unconsciously indicating, the* SERGEANT *counts off seven chairs.* ESSIE *and* SEBASTIAN *indicate to each other that they've got this number:* SEBASTIAN, *smoothing his hair as a signal,* ESSIE *nodding*) I do hope they let you stay for our performance, Ducky. We have the same vibrations. You have the kind of mind I like to read.

SERGEANT JAVORSKY
(*Interested, but not convinced*)
Oh, do you think you could read my mind?

SEBASTIAN

Well, we'll try. Place your mind in the dining room for a moment. (*The* SERGEANT *closes his eyes.*)

SERGEANT JAVORSKY

I'm in the dining room.

ESSIE

I see—seven people. Am I right?

SERGEANT JAVORSKY
(*Opening his eyes*)
Yes, Madame! Exactly right!

78

SEBASTIAN

Now concentrate on the name of one of the guests. Now think hard—

(*The* SERGEANT *closes his eyes again.*)

ESSIE

(*Watching him*)

I have the impression—of an N. (*The* SERGEANT *nods his head, almost unconsciously*)—and a Y. . . (*Again the* SERGEANT *nods*) These seem to come at the end of the name. Could it be—T—NY? (*The* SERGEANT *is immobile*)—R?—NY? (*The* SERGEANT *nods imperceptibly*) Now I see the full name. C-E-R-N-Y. Cerny.

(*The* SERGEANT *opens his eyes with suprise;* SEBASTIAN *pulls* ESSIE'S *plate away from her to keep her concentrating on the* SERGEANT.)

SERGEANT JAVORSKY

That's right, Madame! I was thinking of Mr. Cerny!

ESSIE

(*Pulling her plate back from* SEBASTIAN)

He's an official of some sort. I see him at a desk—

SERGEANT JAVORSKY

He's the new Chief of Press Relations.

ESSIE

(*In a partial "trance" again*)

And I see Mrs. Cerny—shimmering in a yellow—

SERGEANT JAVORSKY

Mrs. Cerny is wearing blue.

ESSIE

—a beautiful shimmering yellow aura all about her. She must be a lovely person. Are you sure she's in blue?

SERGEANT JAVORSKY

I think so.

SEBASTIAN

Now think of another name.
(*The* SERGEANT *closes his eyes again.*)

ESSIE

Oh, this is very clear. N-O-V-O-T-N-Y. Novotny.

SERGEANT JAVORSKY

No, Madame, you're wrong! I wasn't thinking of Mr. Novotny, I was thinking of Mr. Pavlat!

ESSIE

Oh? Mr. Pavlat?

SEBASTIAN
(*To the* SERGEANT)

This can happen, you know. Mr. Novotny has made a deeper impression on you than Mr. Pavlat. That's why Mr. Novotny's name lay deeper in your mind.

ESSIE
(*Innocently*)

Mr. Novotny's a more important man than Mr. Pavlat, isn't he?

SERGEANT JAVORSKY

I can't be sure. Nobody knows exactly what Mr. Pavlat is.

ESSIE

I thought so; negative vibrations.

SEBASTIAN

Is that what the General wants us to find out—what Mr. Pavlat is?

SERGEANT JAVORSKY

I don't know.

SEBASTIAN
(Lightly)
Well, he wants us to find out something. Do you happen to know what it is?

SERGEANT JAVORSKY

You couldn't read the General's mind?

ESSIE
(Changing the subject)
Pavlat. I see a tall blond man. . . .

SERGEANT JAVORSKY

No, no, no, Madame. That's not Mr. Pavlat.

ESSIE

No?

SERGEANT JAVORSKY

Mr. Pavlat is bald.

ESSIE and SEBASTIAN

Bald?

SERGEANT JAVORSKY

Mr. Novotny is tall—

ESSIE

Tall?

SERGEANT JAVORSKY

—and dark.

ESSIE and SEBASTIAN

Tall and dark.
(They are looking and nodding knowingly at each other as they glean each bit of information.)

SERGEANT JAVORSKY

But there is a tall blond woman! And I can see how you made the mistake. Sitting there at the table she looks like a man. She's in uniform. She's on the General's staff. Colonel Bradacova.

ESSIE and SEBASTIAN

Colonel Bradacova!

SEBASTIAN

Oh, it's a cozy little party—(ESSIE *echoes the last names as* SEBASTIAN *says them*) The General, Colonel Bradacova, Mr. Pavlat, Mr. and Mrs. Cerny, Mr. and Mrs. Novotny—

SERGEANT JAVORSKY

No, no, no—she's not exactly Mrs. Novotny—although, in a way—

ESSIE

Ah ha! . . . her!
(*She says this knowingly, then pauses, as if waiting for the name.*)

SERGEANT JAVORSKY

Miss Habova!

ESSIE and SEBASTIAN
(*To each other*)

Habova! . . .

SERGEANT JAVORSKY

Vlasta Habova—

ESSIE and SEBASTIAN

Vlasta Habova! . . .

SERGEANT JAVORSKY

—head of the Cultural Action Committee.

ESSIE
(Coldly resuming her eating)
Those racketeers.

SERGEANT JAVORSKY
(Stepping toward them)
May—may I say something to you in confidence?

SEBASTIAN
(Alert)
About one of the guests?
(The SERGEANT hesitates.)

ESSIE
Come on, Ducky.

SERGEANT JAVORSKY
I like you. I feel I should warn you. You are in danger. (SEBASTIAN *rises*) You are in grave danger. (SEBASTIAN *and* ESSIE *both look concerned*) You will have to use your wits.

SEBASTIAN
(Relieved)
You had me frightened for a minute.
(Relaxed, he sits down again.)

SERGEANT JAVORSKY
I overheard Miss Habova while I was serving cocktails. The Cultural Action people suspect you of trying to smuggle money out of the country. You will be searched—probably at the border.

SEBASTIAN
Thank you. You are very kind, but they will find no money.

ESSIE
You're a nice man, Ducky.

83

SERGEANT JAVORSKY

If you're afraid of trouble at the border, I have friends there—I can give you their names.

ESSIE

That's ever so nice of you— (*Turning to the* SERGEANT) As a matter of fact—

SEBASTIAN

(*Interrupting quickly*)

You know, that was very good caviar—not too salty. But it always makes me so thirsty!

SERGEANT JAVORSKY

Of course! They're having champagne! (*He starts out*) I'll try to get hold of a bottle.

SEBASTIAN

What year?

SERGEANT JAVORSKY

I'll have to look.

SEBASTIAN

Well, bring it anyway. (*The* SERGEANT *exits.* SEBASTIAN *rises, speaks sotto voce but sharply to* ESSIE) Give me your compact!

ESSIE

I wasn't going to tell him—!

SEBASTIAN

Give me your compact!

ESSIE

(*Fumbling in her purse*)

They'll never find it—

SEBASTIAN

They're not going to find it on you!

ESSIE

Please, Rudi!

SEBASTIAN

It's not going to be found on you!

ESSIE
(Handing him the compact)
You'll only tear it up.

SEBASTIAN

No. I promise you.
(He opens the compact, fishes out the stamp.)

ESSIE

Where are you going to hide it? (SEBASTIAN *takes out a package of American cigarettes*) In with the cigarettes?

SEBASTIAN

(As he puts it between the tinfoil and the package cover)
No. There. It'll do for now.

ESSIE

I wish this was over.

SEBASTIAN

Essie, don't worry. Think how much we know already. We'll scare the hell out of these fat cats and get out of here.
(He puts the cigarette pack back in his pocket, puts the plates, silver and napkins on the tray.)

ESSIE

I did have an idea for an opening. . . .

SEBASTIAN

An opening? Good!

ESSIE

I did it once with Alexander.

SEBASTIAN

(Crossing down right)

Let's think of something else.

ESSIE

You haven't even heard it, yet!

SEBASTIAN

If it's Alexander's, I don't want to hear it.

ESSIE

Now listen, Rudi—you bring me in blindfolded and I introduce you to all the ladies in the room by their names.

SEBASTIAN

How're you going to code that?

ESSIE

The color code. . . ! We know Mrs. Cerny's in blue—Colonel Bradacova, she's in uniform—that's gray—you throw me the color and I'll tell you who it is.

SEBASTIAN

(Sits)

Sounds good! But we'd better find out what that Miss Habova is wearing. All right! Let's run the color code. "Madame, will you present me—"

ESSIE

Red.

SEBASTIAN

"Madame, will you be good enough to—"

ESSIE

Gray.

SEBASTIAN
"Madame, may I have the pleasure—"

ESSIE
Blue.

SEBASTIAN
"Madame, may I have the honor—" (*Seeing the* SERGEANT *entering, he trails off into song*) "—of this dance with you? . . ."

ESSIE
(*Singing*)
". . . No, I really would rather not! . . ."
  (*The* SERGEANT *has two champagne glasses and a bottle of champagne. He puts them on the table, fills the two glasses.*)

SERGEANT JAVORSKY
Bollinger, 1934!

SEBASTIAN
Well, why not! We're really thirsty.

ESSIE
(*To the* SERGEANT)
He doesn't know one year from another, Ducky. (*Sips champagne*)
Whooo! I hope we have time to finish the bottle.

SERGEANT JAVORSKY
You will, Madame. They just served the mocha torte.

ESSIE
Oh, you peeked in the dining room?

SERGEANT JAVORSKY
Yes. Mrs. Cerny is wearing blue.

SEBASTIAN

And Miss Habova, of course, is dressed for cultural action?

SERGEANT JAVORSKY

Well, she's dressed for action.

ESSIE

Not—cultural?

SERGEANT JAVORSKY

She looks like some sort of—flamingo.

ESSIE

Flamingo?

SEBASTIAN

(*Choking on the champagne*)

You know, I wasn't prepared for flamingo. . . .

ESSIE

Flamingo. That's a sort of a—pinky-red. Red covers it.

SERGEANT JAVORSKY

It doesn't quite cover Miss Habova.

(*He crosses down right and below the desk to pick up the tray.*)

ESSIE

He's a scream! We like you, Ducky!

ZANDEK

(*Off right*)

Javorsky!

SERGEANT JAVORSKY

You'll excuse me!

(*He starts out, stands at attention in the arch as* ZANDEK *enters.*)

ZANDEK

(Seeing the plates of food)
Get that out of here! You take a lot on yourself, don't you! Get out.
And close the door.

SERGEANT JAVORSKY

Yes, sir.
(He exits, closing the sliding doors.)

ZANDEK

(Going to the desk)
Madame Sebastian, Sebastian. I am glad you are here.

ESSIE and SEBASTIAN

Well, thank you.

ZANDEK

You are about to meet some very important people. Now, let me
tell you who my guests are.

SEBASTIAN

No, General. Let us tell you who your guests are.

ZANDEK

Yes?

SEBASTIAN

(Rising)
Well, not at the moment. But with your permission, General,
Madame and I will wait in that anteroom. And when your guests are
assembled, you will let us know, and I will lead in Madame, blind-
folded.
(He takes ESSIE's hand and leads her to the center of the room.)

ESSIE

And I will introduce Sebastian to each lady in the room, calling
her by name. Remember, General, blindfolded.

SEBASTIAN

Then I will introduce Madame to the gentlemen in the room, calling them by name.

ZANDEK

It is not necessary, all this hocus-pocus. Now! Let me tell you why you are here.
(ESSIE *sits down left.*)

SEBASTIAN

We have been informed that we are here to entertain.

ZANDEK

A little more than that, I hope. (*He sits at the desk*) Give me your attention. Tonight in your dressing room, something happened—

ESSIE

Yes?

ZANDEK

No matter. This is important to me. I have decided to let you try something.

SEBASTIAN
(*Moving toward* ZANDEK)

Try what?

ZANDEK

What I am going to tell you must go no further. It would be dangerous for you if it did. I warn you. Things have been happening to make me suspect—more than suspect. . . . I am quite certain . . . that among those you will meet here tonight is someone who is disloyal.

SEBASTIAN
(*Going to the desk*)

Disloyal to the government?

90

ZANDEK

To me. It is the same thing. (*He rises*) And you are here to find out for me which one it is.

SEBASTIAN

Then, General, it is more important than ever that we use this opening, this introduction—this what you call "hocus-pocus."

ZANDEK

Why?

SEBASTIAN

If you want us to find out what you want us to find out, we must first convince your guests that we can read their minds. Then what will happen?

ZANDEK

What?

SEBASTIAN

If any one of your guests has a guilty thought, he will be frightened —afraid that his thought will betray him.

ZANDEK

My guests are not fools.

SEBASTIAN

General, have you ever tried to keep out of your mind something you're trying to keep out of your mind? You can't do it.

ZANDEK

That's nonsense.

SEBASTIAN

(*Turning to* ESSIE)
Shall I explain to him what I mean?

ESSIE

Why not?

SEBASTIAN

You think it's safe?

ESSIE

Go on. Tell him.

SEBASTIAN

(*Turning back to* ZANDEK)

General, would you like to turn lead into gold? We have the formula . . . it's an old alchemist's formula. (ZANDEK *sits again at the desk*) Put some lead in a pot, place it over a fire, and when it begins to melt . . . (*Gesturing stirring with his hand*) . . . stir slowly—without thinking of the word "rhinoceros." Now that you know the formula, do you think that you could ever stir molten lead without thinking of the word "rhinoceros"?

ZANDEK

You are more intelligent than I thought you were.

SEBASTIAN

We are not the Great Sebastians for nothing.

ESSIE

We are tonight!

ZANDEK

My guests will soon be ready. Is there anything you need?

SEBASTIAN

Yes, some pads and pencils.

ZANDEK

Pads and pencils?

SEBASTIAN

Yes. We will ask each of your guests to write down a thought; then Madame, without seeing what they have written, will read that thought.

ZANDEK

(*Eagerly*)

Can I write something?

SEBASTIAN

Of course.

ZANDEK

And you will read it—out loud?

ESSIE

Word for word.

ZANDEK

That is good. When you read what I will write—I'll be watching their faces. Then I will know. I'll take care of that immediately. (*He opens the sliding doors*) Javorsky!
(*He exits, right.*)

SEBASTIAN

Essie, remember back in the dressing room, when he said, "Not three on a match"—I knew he was a pigeon! This is going to be like shooting fish in a barrel.

ESSIE

We may turn out to be the fish. Rudi, how are we going to get out of this?

SEBASTIAN

It's simple. We'll give a short show, we'll find out that no one is disloyal, and we'll find out in time to pack and catch the seven o'clock train.

ESSIE

I'll be a lot happier when we're on it. I'll be happier when we're home. I'm nervous—let's run the opening.

SEBASTIAN

All right—blue!

ESSIE

Mrs. Cerny.

SEBASTIAN

Gray.

ESSIE

Gray?

SEBASTIAN

You know, the uniform.

ESSIE

Colonel Bradacova.

SEBASTIAN

Red. Flamingo.

ESSIE

That bitch.

SEBASTIAN

Habova.

ESSIE

Habova, Habova, Habova!

SEBASTIAN

Now, the men. Short and glasses with a ribbon.

ESSIE

Mr. Cerny.

SEBASTIAN

Tall and dark.

94

ESSIE

Mr. Novotny. That's the man with the dentist's bill. Mr. Nov— (*The* SERGEANT *enters with pads and pencils.* SEBASTIAN *doesn't see him but* ESSIE *does, and starts singing a cockney tune*) "Oh, your hat don't fit you very well—"

SERGEANT JAVORSKY

You wanted these?

SEBASTIAN

Yes, just put them on the desk, please.
　(*He does.*)

SERGEANT JAVORSKY

The General tells me you are to wait in the anteroom until his guests are ready for you.

ESSIE

That's right, Ducky.

SERGEANT JAVORSKY

You may have to wait in there for some time. The General doesn't want to start until all the guests have arrived.

SEBASTIAN
(*Moving toward him*)

All the guests?

SERGEANT JAVORSKY

There's another couple coming.

SEBASTIAN
(*Worried*)

Another couple?

ESSIE
(*Rising and joining* SEBASTIAN)
Who are they, Ducky?

SERGEANT JAVORSKY

The General didn't say.
(*He exits, right.*)

SEBASTIAN

(*Turning to* ESSIE)
There goes your sensational opening!

ESSIE

How was I to know?

SEBASTIAN

I knew it the minute you mentioned Alexander.

ESSIE

Anyway, we know what three of them are wearing.

SEBASTIAN

Well, if one of the ladies comes in naked, at least we'll know she's the fourth.

ESSIE

Whatever she's wearing, leave her till the last.

SEBASTIAN

And when you introduce me, what name are you going to give—Lady Godiva?
(*They both turn and start toward the anteroom.* ZANDEK *enters.*)

ZANDEK

We are leaving the table. If you wish to surprise them—
(*He indicates the anteroom.*)

SEBASTIAN

General, you know that opening, that introduction we mentioned? You were right, it is hocus-pocus.

ESSIE

We'd better not do it.

ZANDEK

No, I like it very much! I want you to do it!

SEBASTIAN

No, General.

ESSIE

We'll have to think of something else.

ZANDEK

But I have already told my guests. They are expecting it!

ESSIE

No, General, we're sorry.
(*The* SERGEANT *enters with an extra chair which he places against the wall, below the Chinese cabinet.*)

ZANDEK

One moment. (*Turns to* JAVORSKY) Javorsky, be sure to save some supper for Dr. and Mrs. Balzar.

SERGEANT JAVORSKY

Dr. and Mrs. Balzar. Yes, sir.
(*He exits, right.* ESSIE *and* SEBASTIAN *exchange glances.*)

ZANDEK

(*Turning back to the* SEBASTIANS)
All right, all right. If you don't want to do it, don't do it.

ESSIE

But we do want to do it!

97

SEBASTIAN

We insist on doing it!

ZANDEK
(*Bewildered*)
I don't understand you people!

ESSIE
(*As she opens the door to the anteroom*)
That's good!

SEBASTIAN

That's very good!
(*They exit into the anteroom.* VLASTA HABOVA *and* COLONEL JARKA BRADACOVA *enter from up right, followed by* SOPHIE CERNY.)

COLONEL BRADACOVA

Oh, it was not difficult at all. It's only a two-hour drive. I made it in plenty of time. (*Seeing* ZANDEK, *she goes to him*) Otokar, don't let the men stay in the dining room all night. That's very undemocratic.

SOPHIE
(*To* HABOVA)
I've been admiring your dress all evening. May I ask where you got it?

VLASTA HABOVA

It came from Paris.

ZANDEK
(*Offering the* COLONEL *a cigarette from his case*)
Cigarette?
(*The* COLONEL *takes one.*)

COLONEL BRADACOVA

Thank you.
(*Takes out her lighter and lights her cigarette.*)

SOPHIE

Karel tells me we won't have any more French fashions for a long time.

VLASTA HABOVA

Oh, the French are being difficult. They'll get over it. Show a Frenchman a franc—he'll find a way of getting it.

COLONEL BRADACOVA

Otokar, Lieutenant Stanicek has asked for twenty-four hours' leave, starting Wednesday midnight. Is it all right?

ZANDEK

Yes. Things are quiet again. (*Looks around at table, down left*) Where's the coffee? The coffee should be here. Excuse me. (*He starts out*) Javorsky!
(*He exits up right.*)

COLONEL BRADACOVA
(*Turning to them*)
I thought you girls were going upstairs!

SOPHIE

I am. (*She starts for stairs, turns back, stops*) Oh! I have never seen such a supper! Where does the General get all that food? This morning I stood in line for two hours, just to buy some butter.

COLONEL BRADACOVA

You stood in line?

VLASTA HABOVA

Why should you stand in line?

SOPHIE

Oh, I wouldn't want to take advantage of my husband's position in the government.

VLASTA HABOVA

What!
(BRADACOVA *and* HABOVA *exchange a look*.)

SOPHIE

Oh, I don't mind standing in line—it's just the time it takes. What with the children and the entertaining back and forth and all those Party meetings; if I didn't have to go to all those Party meetings—

VLASTA HABOVA

Oh, I see. The things you like to do least are "those Party meetings!" They are the big waste of time, eh?

SOPHIE

You misunderstood me—that's not what I meant at all!

COLONEL BRADACOVA

Sophie, never mind.

VLASTA HABOVA

You said it, didn't you? You don't like to go to Party meetings.

COLONEL BRADACOVA

Vlasta!

SOPHIE

My husband is a Party member!

COLONEL BRADACOVA

Sophie, don't.

SOPHIE

Do you think for one minute I would criticize the Party?
(ZANDEK *enters*.)

VLASTA HABOVA

You just don't care about the Party. It's too much trouble.

SOPHIE

It is very dangerous, now, to accuse people of indifference.

VLASTA HABOVA
(*Turning on her*)
It is dangerous today to talk too much.

COLONEL BRADACOVA

Vlasta!

VLASTA HABOVA
(*Glaring at* SOPHIE)
You talk too much!

COLONEL BRADACOVA

Quiet! We've had enough of this!

VLASTA HABOVA

I am not a soldier in your outfit, Jarka.
(SOPHIE *has started upstairs. She pauses and looks over the rail.*)

SOPHIE

Well, is anyone else coming upstairs?
(*There is no answer, and she continues on up, giving a frightened look behind her.*)

ZANDEK
(*Crossing to* HABOVA)
What was all that about?

VLASTA HABOVA

You know Sophie Cerny. She's a fool.

COLONEL BRADACOVA

Now, Vlasta!

ZANDEK

She's unimportant.
(The SERGEANT *enters and crosses down left, followed by the* THIRD SOLDIER, *who is carrying a large silver tray on which are the demitasse cups and a silver coffee urn. The* THIRD SOLDIER *puts the tray on the table and stands behind it.)*

COLONEL BRADACOVA

Otokar, that was a good supper!

ZANDEK

Better than the officers' mess!

COLONEL BRADACOVA

Oh, yes!

VLASTA HABOVA

And this house! You've done very well for yourself.

ZANDEK
(Brusquely)
This house was assigned to me by the Confiscation Commission!

VLASTA HABOVA
(Placatingly)
Otokar, I did not mean it that way—why, of course you deserve a house like this! I envy you. I used to envy the Bileks, when they lived here.

COLONEL BRADACOVA

The Bileks?

VLASTA HABOVA

The Jan Bileks.

COLONEL BRADACOVA

Oh, the mining family! They lived here?

ZANDEK

Until nationalization.

VLASTA HABOVA

On my way to work—at the factory—I used to pass by this house. The grounds— (*Indicating windows*) with the high wall. I hated them for not letting me see over that wall.

ZANDEK

You did, eh? You can see now. The land goes all the way down to the river.

VLASTA HABOVA

I'd like to walk on those grounds.

ZANDEK

(*Opening the iron grille and windows*)
Go ahead. We're waiting for the Balzars. (*The women start out*) Wait. Colonel, you'd better go first. (*To* HABOVA) The guards. (*To* BRADACOVA) Have them show Vlasta around.
(*The women disappear through the window, and we hear a whistle from one of the soldiers, off.*)

COLONEL BRADACOVA

(*Off*)

It's all right.
(MR. CERNY *enters. He is short, wearing glasses with a ribbon. He glances nervously around the room.*)

CERNY

Where's Sophie?

ZANDEK

She's upstairs.

CERNY

She's all right?

ZANDEK

Oh, yes.

CERNY

Poor Sophie. . . . She's very eager—but with five children, who can be politically minded?

ZANDEK
(Indicating the coffee)
Coffee?
(They cross to the table, left. The THIRD SOLDIER *has poured two cups, handing one to each.* CERNY *sits in the chair right of table. We hear the voices of* NOVOTNY *and* PAVLAT, *off right.)*

NOVOTNY
(Off)
That's one I will try to remember.

PAVLAT
(As they appear in the archway)
I heard it from the Polish minister. He thought it was very funny.
*(*NOVOTNY *is tall and dark,* PAVLAT *bald.)*

NOVOTNY
(As they cross to the coffee)
Strange, you don't hear funny stories any more. Why is that?

PAVLAT

These are serious times. The events of last month have left the people nervous—jumpy.
*(*PAVLAT *takes two cups, hands one to* NOVOTNY.)*

CERNY

The dust is settling.
(*The* SERGEANT *exits, up right.*)

NOVOTNY

Thanks to you, Cerny. You did a good job. The press was well handled.

CERNY

I was hoping for a better press abroad.
(PAVLAT *circles up and across to right center.*)

NOVOTNY

It was not too bad, considering.

CERNY

It was not good. Some of them openly accused us of—doing what we did.

ZANDEK

(*Suspiciously*)
Do you disapprove of what we did?

CERNY

(*Rising*)
For God's sake, Zandek—don't you trust anybody?

NOVOTNY

We did not expect the West to be pleased. Gentlemen! For a little while, nothing else must happen. That's why I feel we must keep Masaryk in office. It is important. Don't you think so, Pavlat?

PAVLAT

Masaryk is a symbol.

ZANDEK

You think we need that symbol?

PAVLAT

At present, yes. (*Drawing himself up, turning to* ZANDEK, *as he senses some disagreement*) I will defend that point of view!

CERNY

We need prestige abroad. They're bound to respect a regime of which Masaryk is Foreign Minister.

ZANDEK

I'm still not sure of him. All through the February events, I had him watched.

PAVLAT

He will go along. He has to.
(*He leans against the edge of the desk.* COLONEL BRADACOVA *and* VLASTA HABOVA *enter from the French windows,* BRADACOVA *closing them behind them.*)

VLASTA HABOVA

Who will go along?

CERNY

Masaryk.

VLASTA HABOVA

He's weak.
(*She sits in the chair at the desk.* SOPHIE *enters down the stairs in time to hear some of this conversation.*)

SOPHIE
(*Coming into the room*)
Oh, dear—are you still talking politics?

CERNY
(*Warning*)
Sophie!

THE GREAT SEBASTIANS

SOPHIE

(Alarmed, covering quickly, as she goes to him)
Not that it's not important! I just meant—the General said we were
to have some entertainment. We were to have our palms read.

CERNY

Not palms, Sophie. Minds!

SOPHIE

Minds! Oh, do we have to?
(She sits near the table. CERNY *returns his empty cup and gets
a cup for* SOPHIE.)

VLASTA HABOVA

Oh, yes, the Sebastians. Haven't they come?
(NOVOTNY *takes a cup of coffee to* HABOVA.)

ZANDEK

They are here. They are waiting.
(COLONEL BRADACOVA *has finished closing the grille door, locks
it and stands near it.)*

VLASTA HABOVA

If you had asked me, Otokar, I would have advised you not to have
them.

ZANDEK

You don't want your mind read?

VLASTA HABOVA

As far as my Committee is concerned, they are not in good favor.

NOVOTNY

(To ZANDEK*)*
You don't really believe they can read minds!

ZANDEK

Well, they do some things that are not easy to explain.

PAVLAT

Of course they can't read minds. If they could, it would be dangerous.

ZANDEK

Why should it be dangerous? (*His glance sweeps the room*) Is there
anyone here who objects to having his mind read?
(*There is a murmur of conversation from the guests.*)

VLASTA HABOVA

Why should we? It's just a trick.

CERNY

Let's start.
(*The doorbell rings.*)

ZANDEK

That must be the Balzars.

SOPHIE

I like the Balzars. No one else coming?
(SERGEANT JAVORSKY *is seen crossing the arch to answer the
door.*)

ZANDEK

I wanted to have Babicka, but I couldn't reach him.

VLASTA HABOVA

Babicka?
(*There is a sudden silence.*)

PAVLAT

General, was Babicka a close friend of yours?

ZANDEK

(*Looking from one guest to another*)
I've known him for years.

PAVLAT

I would no longer mention that if I were you.
(*A sudden pall falls over the room.*)

ZANDEK
(*To himself, aloud*)

Babicka!
(*He goes up into the hall and off left, as offstage voices are heard.*)

SERGEANT JAVORSKY
(*Off*)

Good evening. Come right in.

BALZAR
(*Off*)

Is the party over?

MARIE BALZAR
(*Off*)

I hope everyone hasn't gone!

BALZAR
(*Off*)

Here we are, Otokar. We made it!

MARIE

Tani will tell you it's all my fault—and it is! (*The* BALZARS *are young, attractive. She wears a long evening coat. They make their way among the guests, greeting, shaking hands.* SOPHIE *has risen and crossed up to greet* MARIE) Sophie!

BALZAR
(*Coming into the room*)

I'm sorry we're late. These days it's hard to get away from the office. Novotny!
(*Shaking his hand. The* SERGEANT *puts* BALZAR'S *coat and hat on the bench and exits, off right.*)

MARIE
(*Crossing to* HABOVA)
Vlasta! Hello!

BALZAR
(*Crossing to* PAVLAT, *shakes his hand*)
Then I had to pick up Marie—

MARIE
Colonel!

COLONEL BRADACOVA
How do you do!
(ZANDEK *returns to the room.*)

BALZAR
—And Marie—you know Marie— (*Shakes* CERNY's *hand, crosses to center*)—in the three years we have been married, she is already five years late! (*He is now facing his wife, crossing to her*)—which is why you look so young, darling.
(*He goes to her and takes her hand.*)

ZANDEK
No matter. You are still in time.

MARIE
In time for what?

COLONEL BRADACOVA
Otokar has that mind-reading act here from the Variété.

ZANDEK
Would you like some supper, first?

BALZAR
No, thank you, we are not at all hungry.

MARIE

Speak for yourself. (*To herself*) Did I have any dinner? I don't remember!

ZANDEK

Javorsky—a plate of food for Mrs. Balzar.

MARIE

(*As* ZANDEK *helps her out of her coat*)
Go right ahead. I can eat and have my mind read at the same time. (*As she removes her coat, we see she is wearing a gown of the exact shade of blue as that worn by* MRS. CERNY. *The* THIRD SOLDIER *crosses to* ZANDEK, *takes* MARIE'S *coat, puts it on the hall bench and exits, off right.* MARIE *goes and sits on the piano stool next to* SOPHIE CERNY.)

ZANDEK

Is everybody ready? I'll see if we can start. (*He goes to the anteroom, knocks, opens the door*) Are you ready?

SEBASTIAN
(*Off, sotto voce*)
Yes.

ZANDEK
(*Turning to the others*)
Attention, everybody! Mr. and Mrs. Sebastian! (*He and* COLONEL BRADACOVA *applaud. A hoarse whisper from the anteroom is heard.* ZANDEK *goes to the anteroom door, then returns*) I beg your pardon! —The Great Sebastians!
(*They all applaud as the* SEBASTIANS *make a highly theatrical entrance,* SEBASTIAN *holding* ESSIE'S *right hand high in the air.* ESSIE *is blindfolded. He parades her down center and then turns left and suddenly stops as he finds himself facing the two women in the same shade of blue, sitting beside each other. Hastily, he backs up, turns and leads the startled* ESSIE—*with great aplomb—toward stage right, stopping when he reaches* COLONEL BRADACOVA.)

SEBASTIAN

(*To* ESSIE)

Madame Sebastian, will you be good enough to present me?

ESSIE

Colonel Bradacova, may I introduce the Great Sebastian.
(SEBASTIAN *bows.*)

COLONEL BRADACOVA

(*Astonished and delighted*)

How did she know?

VLASTA HABOVA

It's just a trick!

SEBASTIAN

(*Turning* ESSIE *to confront* HABOVA)

Madame, will you present me?

ESSIE

Miss Habova, this is the Great Sebastian.

VLASTA HABOVA

It's just a trick!

NOVOTNY

(*Laughing*)

Well, you have to admit it's a damn good trick!

SEBASTIAN

(*Forced to move on to his dilemma, the two ladies in blue—and think-ing fast now*)

And now, Madame—these two ladies—may I have the pleasure—the double pleasure?

ESSIE

(*Paralyzed for a moment, then freeing her hand of* SEBASTIAN'S, *she extends it vaguely in the direction of the women*)

How do you do, Mrs. Cerny?

SOPHIE

(Pleased, she impulsively rises and takes ESSIE's *hand)*
Oh! How do you do!

ESSIE

(Turning smoothly to Sebastian)
This is a pleasure! May I introduce the Great Sebastian.

SOPHIE

Karel! Did you hear! She is wonderful!
(She goes to her husband as SEBASTIAN *turns in triumph and relief to* MRS. BALZAR.)*

SEBASTIAN

And again the pleasure?

ESSIE

Mrs. Balzar. The Great Sebastian.

MARIE

Touché!
(She rises, goes to her husband, as ESSIE *whips off her blindfold and they all applaud.)*

SEBASTIAN

(Indicating the men as he speaks)
And now it is my privilege. Madame Sebastian, may I present Dr. Balzar—

ESSIE

How do you do?
*(*BALZAR *bows.)*

SEBASTIAN

(Turning her toward each man as he introduces him)
Mr. Cerny—

ESSIE

How do you do?

SEBASTIAN

The General you know—

ESSIE

Oh, yes.

SEBASTIAN

Mr. Pavlat—

ESSIE

How do you do?

SEBASTIAN

And—Mr. Novotny.
(SERGEANT JAVORSKY *enters and stands at the right of the arch.*)

ESSIE

How do you do?

NOVOTNY

Madame.
(*There is conversational murmur and applause.* SOPHIE *sits on the loveseat.*)

SEBASTIAN

(*Standing with* ESSIE *left of center, their backs to the footlights*)
Ladies and gentlemen! May we have your attention? (*The chatter dies*) It is Madame's great gift that she can read your thoughts.

SOPHIE

(*Putting her hand to her mouth*)
Oh, please!

SEBASTIAN

Thoughts are like images on a photographic plate. (*He goes to* SOPHIE) Sometimes they fade swiftly— (*He turns to* ZANDEK) —at others they remain forever. (*He comes back to* ESSIE) In order to help you concentrate, we shall ask each of you to write a thought on a piece of paper. (*Turns to the* SERGEANT) Sergeant, would you see that each guest is provided with a pad and pencil.

(The SERGEANT *takes pads and pencils and passes them during the following dialogue—first, to the* CERNYS, *then to the* BALZARS, *then* PAVLAT, *then* ZANDEK. *Then he moves up and stands right of the arch. At the same time,* NOVOTNY, VLASTA HABOVA *and* COLONEL BRADACOVA *get their pads and pencils from the desk.)*

SEBASTIAN

Now, ladies and gentlemen. When you have written your thought, please fold the paper twice—fold the paper twice—and I will collect them in that bowl.

(Indicating a bowl on the piano, he starts for it; PAVLAT *gets it and hands it to him.)*

BALZAR

Mr. Sebastian, don't read my mind in the presence of my wife!

MARIE

I can read your mind better than he can!

SEBASTIAN

Please write down a thought—

MARIE

But I can't think of a thought!

ZANDEK

Put down anything! Don't delay the game.

*(*CERNY *and* SOPHIE *go to* ESSIE.)*

CERNY

Madame Sebastian—instead of writing a thought, may I write a question?

*(*SEBASTIAN *has started to collect the slips, constantly watching* ESSIE.)*

ESSIE

I do not answer questions. I am not clairvoyant. (*As* CERNY *bows and turns away, she suddenly assumes her faraway expression*) But I have an impression of why you want to ask a question. (*The* CERNYS *turn back to her*) You are worried. Something is constantly on your mind. An illness?

SOPHIE

Karel—you know!

CERNY

Shhh!

ESSIE

Not yours—a relative, perhaps?

CERNY

Which relative?

SOPHIE

Karel! It's your father!

CERNY

Sophie!

ESSIE

(*Pretending not to notice* SOPHIE's *slip, she puts her right hand to her closed eyelids and "concentrates"*)
It is your father. He is ill—in hospital. Not here in Prague. Think of the village where he is. (*Hesitates, then*) Oh, this is not a village. It's a town—a very large one—I see roofs and roofs and roofs! I have the impression—of a B.—Bratislava.

SOPHIE

Karel! She is wonderful! (*Turning to the others*) Isn't she marvelous? It's all true, you know!

116

VLASTA HABOVA

Oh, it's just a trick!

NOVOTNY

Vlasta! (*To* ESSIE) Madame, you are quite remarkable!

ESSIE

Thank you!

VLASTA HABOVA
(*To* NOVOTNY)

Ask her to tell you something about yourself. (*Challenging* ESSIE) Tell him something!

SEBASTIAN

(*Passing elaborately near* ESSIE, *collecting slips from* NOVOTNY *and the* COLONEL) Don't hesitate, Madame. . . . Tell Mr. Novotny something. No hesitation. . . .

ESSIE
(*Moving to* NOVOTNY)

I have the impression, Mr. Novotny, that you are happier than you were a short while ago.

NOVOTNY

Vlasta, that is a compliment to you!

ESSIE
(*Looking over her shoulder at* HABOVA)

No—it is not her—(*She looks back at* NOVOTNY)—It is your teeth! You no longer have trouble with your teeth.

NOVOTNY
(*Confounded*)

Vlasta—you know I *have* had— (*Turning to* ZANDEK) General, these people are amazing!

ZANDEK

I told you before, they do things that are not easy to explain.

SEBASTIAN

(*Having collected the last paper from* HABOVA)

And now, General, we would like to have you all on the other side of the room. Would you please all go to the other side of the room—

ZANDEK

(*Crosses up left*)

Colonel, everybody—this side!
(*There is general chatter as the guests move to the left side of the room.*)

COLONEL BRADACOVA

(*To* HABOVA)

Vlasta, I have never seen these people before, and they knew my name!
(*As the group has moved to re-arrange itself stage left,* SEBASTIAN *and* ESSIE *have stood shoulder to shoulder, downstage right, their backs somewhat to the audience,* SEBASTIAN *holding the bowl in his left hand.* ESSIE *is on his left. He reaches his right hand behind his back toward her. In it, we see palmed a folded slip of paper. With her right hand, she takes this paper and, with the help of her left hand, unfolds it behind her back.*)

SEBASTIAN

(*Moving up center*)

Madame Sebastian, by pressing your written thought against her forehead, still folded and invisible, will tell you what you have written. (*He puts the bowl on the desk*) And now—in order to help Madame concentrate, I must ask you all, please, to be very, very, quiet. (*Suddenly he stamps his foot and—as though very annoyed and angry—starts for the hall*) Is there someone out there in the hall?
(*The* GENERAL *and* JAVORSKY *move swiftly up into the arch; all eyes follow them and there is excited chatter. This diversion allows* ESSIE *to turn and read, quite deliberately, and in full view of the audience, what is written on the slip of paper she holds.*)

ZANDEK

There is no one here! (*He turns to the* SERGEANT) Javorsky, see that we are not disturbed. Close the doors.

(*The* SERGEANT *exits and does so.* ESSIE *sits at the desk, the bowl before her.* SEBASTIAN *comes down to the corner of the desk. The* GENERAL *has returned to a position near the group.*)

SEBASTIAN

(*Holding his hand up*)

Quiet, please—Madame must concentrate. Madame, we are waiting.

(ESSIE *puts her hand into the bowl and takes out one of the papers, folded, as she slips her original one, crumpled, back into the bowl. She presses the second one to her forehead.*)

ESSIE

(*As if in great concentration*)

"The People's—Democracy—will live—forever."

(*This, of course, is the message that was on the slip she had already read.*)

CERNY

(*Stepping forward*)

But—that is word for word what I wrote!

ESSIE

(*Opening and reading the second paper*)

Yes, word for word.

(*She puts the paper, still opened, back into the bowl and takes a new folded one out, pressing it against her forehead. She "concentrates" again. Meanwhile, there is excited conversation among the guests.*)

VLASTA HABOVA

We all think that all the time, I hope!

SEBASTIAN

Quiet, please! Madame must concentrate!

VLASTA HABOVA

Wait until she gets my thought. She won't dare concentrate on that.

SEBASTIAN

Quiet, please!

ESSIE
(Presses the paper to her forehead)
"Somebody—in this—room—"

ZANDEK

Yes!
(He watches the faces of his guests closely. The doorbell rings.)

ESSIE

"—has revealed—"

ZANDEK

Yes?

ESSIE

"—secret information—"

ZANDEK

Yes—yes—yes— *(There is a knock on the doors, center. They are opened from without by the* SERGEANT. ZANDEK *speaks angrily to the* SERGEANT*)* I told you no one! I will see no one!

SERGEANT JAVORSKY

(Interrupting and coming to attention at the left side of the arch)
I'm sorry, General, but it's Comrade Bacilek!
*(*STEPAN BACILEK *enters from off left. He is a man of authority.)*

BACILEK

General, I have to interrupt!

ZANDEK

Not now! Can't it wait?

BACILEK

No. It cannot wait! (*He turns to the group*) Novotny! Balzar! You are to report at once to the Prime Minister. He is waiting for you. (*He has stepped into the room as he calls the men by name. They start for the center arch.* PAVLAT *rises*) Pavlat, the Foreign Office is talking to Moscow. (NOVOTNY *and* BALZAR *stop and listen to* BACILEK) There will be instructions for you.

PAVLAT

What's happened?

CERNY

Is there trouble?

NOVOTNY

What's wrong?

SOPHIE
(*Rises*)

Karel, what does this mean?

VLASTA HABOVA
(*Rises*)

Yes, what is it?

BALZAR

What has happened?
(*There is a slight pause.*)

ZANDEK

Tell us!

BACILEK
(*Turning to* ZANDEK)

Masaryk is dead.

BALZAR

Dead?

VLASTA HABOVA

Masaryk?

NOVOTNY

Masaryk dead?

PAVLAT
(*Crossing to* BACILEK)

Comrade, how?

BACILEK
(*To* PAVLAT)

Suicide.
(ESSIE *and* SEBASTIAN *listen to the scene ignored by the others.*)

SOPHIE
(*Moved*)
Oh, no—not Masaryk—not suicide!

BACILEK

How else?
(SOPHIE *withdraws, pressing her handkerchief to her lips, her body shaking silently.* BALZAR *and* NOVOTNY *go for their coats on the bench.* PAVLAT *crosses, takes his coat and exits, left.*)

VLASTA HABOVA

I knew he was weak! (*She exits into the anteroom.* MARIE *crosses to* BALZAR *in the hall. He helps her into her evening wrap, and they exit, left.*)

BACILEK

General Zandek, you will be responsible for public order if the news creates any disturbance.

ZANDEK

Yes, Comrade! (*To* COLONEL BRADACOVA) Colonel, we will deploy as on the twenty-third. I will join you later.

COLONEL BRADACOVA

Yes, sir.
(*She exits, off left.* SOPHIE *sinks onto the piano stool.*)

CERNY

Bacilek, what will this mean?

BACILEK

It is too soon to know. It has come at a bad time.

CERNY

I must get to my office. (*Turning to* SOPHIE) Sophie, get your wrap.

BACILEK

Cerny, under no circumstances will there be a release of this news until it has been decided how it is to be announced. (SOPHIE *is sobbing.* CERNY *gives her a worried glance*) How the news is given out is of great importance.

CERNY

Sophie! Please be quiet. (*Her sobbing increases. He goes to her and shakes her, bringing her to her feet*) Sophie, for God's sake! Stop that!

ESSIE

Let her cry! Why shouldn't she cry?
(BACILEK *realizes the presence of the* SEBASTIANS *for the first time.* SOPHIE *looks at* ESSIE *for reassurance then, still sobbing, hurries off into the anteroom.* HABOVA *enters from the anteroom with her fur jacket on as* SOPHIE *exits into it.*)

VLASTA HABOVA

What's she crying about? Masaryk? He's not worth it!

SEBASTIAN

Mr. Masaryk was a good man.
(HABOVA *tosses her head haughtily, exits into the hall and disappears off left with* NOVOTNY.)

BACILEK

(*His eyes on the* SEBASTIANS)

Who are these people?

SEBASTIAN

It's all right. We were friends of Mr. Masaryk's.

ZANDEK

They are entertainers.
(*The* SERGEANT *has closed the anteroom door and now stands on the step, facing the room.*)

BACILEK

(*To* ZANDEK)

Did they know Masaryk?

SEBASTIAN

Yes. We worked together in London, during the war. We had lunch with him today.

ZANDEK

You were with Masaryk today?

SEBASTIAN

Yes. He was too busy to come to the theatre, so he asked us to have lunch with him.

BACILEK

(*Going to* SEBASTIAN)

What did he talk about?

SEBASTIAN

About London . . . about the war . . . about the old days. . . .

ZANDEK

Was he thinking of suicide?

CERNY

What was his mood?

ESSIE

He wasn't as gay as he used to be—but he wasn't depressed.

SEBASTIAN

He was—*triste*. But I can't believe he would commit suicide.

ESSIE

No one will believe he committed suicide.

BACILEK
(*To* ZANDEK)

That is our problem.

ZANDEK
(*To the* SEBASTIANS)

But you must have sensed something!

SEBASTIAN

General, Mr. Masaryk's death is as great a shock to us as it is to you.

ZANDEK

You had lunch with Masaryk today—he commits suicide tonight— and you noticed nothing? I don't believe you! You lie. Get out of my house. Go!
(ESSIE *gets up slowly and* SEBASTIAN *starts with her toward the anteroom.*)

SERGEANT JAVORSKY
(*With quiet authority*)
One moment. (*They stop*) You are not to go. You will stay.

ZANDEK
(*Turning sharply to* JAVORSKY)
I told them to go!

SERGEANT JAVORSKY
(*Crossing down to* ZANDEK; *just as sharply*)
I told them to stay!
(ESSIE *and* SEBASTIAN *turn and look at* ZANDEK.)

ZANDEK
(*With rising anger*)
Sergeant, you're being insolent!

BACILEK
(*With authority*)
General, you will speak with respect! Comrade Javorsky represents
the Party.
(*There is a stunned silence.* ZANDEK *crosses to the window,
right, and stands, his hands behind his back.*)

CERNY
(*Embarrassed*)
I must get to my office. (*He goes to the anteroom and opens the
door*) Sophie! (*Goes back to* BACILEK) I shall wait to hear from you.
(SOPHIE *hurries out of the anteroom, around through the arch,
and off, left.* CERNY *picks up his coat and follows her.*)

SEBASTIAN
(*To the* SERGEANT)
How long do you want us to stay here?

126

SERGEANT JAVORSKY

I can't tell you that, now. Wait.

SEBASTIAN

But I'm afraid we can't wait. We have a train to catch.
(*They exit into the anteroom, closing the door.*)

SERGEANT JAVORSKY

General, they are not to leave this house.

BACILEK

(*To* JAVORSKY)

What do you want with them?

SERGEANT JAVORSKY

They may be important.

BACILEK

Important?

SERGEANT JAVORSKY

These two were the last outsiders to see Masaryk alive. If there
is to be an announcement that Jan Masaryk committed suicide—a
statement from them telling why—would be very valuable. (*Carefully
planning in his mind*) I could prepare such a statement.

BACILEK

That could be of great service, Comrade.

SERGEANT JAVORSKY

I need the Corporal.
(*He exits through the arch to the right.* ZANDEK *watches him,
off.*)

ZANDEK

Comrade, is my loyalty being questioned?

BACILEK

No, Comrade. Your authority.

ZANDEK

My authority?

BACILEK

This is a political matter. It is out of your hands.

ZANDEK

(*Going to* BACILEK)
Yes, but why was Javorsky put in my house!

BACILEK

You have been in the Party long enough not to ask for explanations.

ZANDEK

But without my knowing who he was!
(*The* SERGEANT *and* CORPORAL *enter in the arch, followed by the* SECOND *and* THIRD SOLDIERS, *who remain at attention in the hall. The* CORPORAL *is carrying a large towel.*)

SERGEANT JAVORSKY

(*To the* CORPORAL; *indicating the desk*)
There!
(*The* CORPORAL *spreads the towel on the upper end of the desk, and steps back at attention.*)

ZANDEK

(*To* BACILEK)
I'll be at headquarters.
(*He starts out.*)

BACILEK

General Zandek. (ZANDEK *stops*) Masaryk had many friends. When the news of his death becomes known, there may be attempts to defect. The border control should be tightened.

ZANDEK

(*Thoughtfully*)

Then I should be in command there myself. I can be at the border by daybreak. For the next hour I shall be at headquarters.

(*He starts off left. The* SEBASTIANS *come out of the anteroom,* ESSIE *carrying her handbag,* SEBASTIAN *their capes.*)

BACILEK

(*Following* ZANDEK)

I'll let you drop me.

(*They exit.*)

SEBASTIAN

(*As they enter*)

Essie, please—pull yourself together. (*To the* SERGEANT) Is there a car that can take us to our hotel?

ESSIE

Yes, all this has made us very late.

(*They start for the arch.*)

SERGEANT JAVORSKY

You are staying here. Don't try to leave this house.

ESSIE

I'd like to know who's going to stop us?

SEBASTIAN

What right have you to hold us?

SERGEANT JAVORSKY

You are under arrest! (*The* SECOND *and* THIRD SOLDIERS *step into the arch to block their way*) You are under suspicion of trying to smuggle money out of Czechoslovakia!

SEBASTIAN

Smuggling?!
(*He drops the capes on a chair.*)

ESSIE

Who says so?

SERGEANT JAVORSKY

Sebastian—empty your pockets! (*He points to the desk*) Madame—
your handbag!

ESSIE

No!

SERGEANT JAVORSKY

If you please!!

ESSIE
(*Automatically*)

Rubber boots!

SEBASTIAN
(*To* ESSIE)

No—!

SERGEANT JAVORSKY

Corporal!
(*The* CORPORAL *strides toward* ESSIE; *she eludes him with a deft
sleight of hand with her bag, then tosses it on the desk.* SEBAS-
TIAN *goes to the desk and empties his pockets, producing a
variety of objects, including his pack of cigarettes.*)

ESSIE
(*To the* SERGEANT)

Who are you, I'd like to know? Pretending to be our friend! Caviar
and roast goose! Butter wouldn't melt in your mouth.

SEBASTIAN

Essie!

ESSIE

Just a dirty sneak, if you want my opinion!

SERGEANT JAVORSKY

Yes, a sneak. But not a fool.

ESSIE

That's your opinion.

SERGEANT JAVORSKY

Corporal, they are to be thoroughly searched: stripped to the skin!

ESSIE

Not my skin! No one's going to strip me to my skin.

SEBASTIAN

Don't think we're going to submit to anything like that.

SERGEANT JAVORSKY

Corporal!

CORPORAL

(*Starting for the arch*)

I'll take them upstairs. Marinska can take the woman, I'll take him.
I'll get her.

(*He exits up the stairs.*)

ESSIE

(*Her eyes have fastened on the pack of cigarettes lying on the desk*)
Rudi—I could do with a cigarette.

(SEBASTIAN *takes the pack, hands her a cigarette.*)

SERGEANT JAVORSKY

Oh, American cigarettes!

SEBASTIAN

Yes, we like American cigarettes.
(*He is about to put the cigarettes in his pocket.*)

SERGEANT JAVORSKY

So do I.
(*He holds out his hand for the cigarettes.* SEBASTIAN *goes to him, tries to give him only one, but the* SERGEANT *takes the pack, removes a cigarette from it, then puts the entire pack in his right jacket pocket.*)

ESSIE

(*Pointing at the disappearing pack*)
Rudi, he's got a bloody nerve, he has! Are you going to—

SEBASTIAN

Quiet! Let me handle this. (*He crosses below the desk to stage center*) Sergeant, we are ready to be searched.

ESSIE

Rudi!

SEBASTIAN

Essie, we have nothing to hide.
(*They exchange a look.* ESSIE *looks back at the* SERGEANT, *smiles, then turns to* SEBASTIAN. SEBASTIAN *offers his arm to her and they start for the stairs, giving a salute to the two* SOLDIERS *as*

The Curtain Falls

ACT THREE

ACT THREE

The scene is the same as Act Two. It is half an hour later.

AT RISE: *The stage is empty. After a pause* SEBASTIAN *comes cautiously down the stairs. He looks back and gestures to* ESSIE, *who is not yet in sight, to stay upstairs. He looks offstage to the right, listens a moment, then disappears offstage left.* ESSIE *comes down the stairs into sight, looking after him. In a moment* SEBASTIAN *returns. They meet at the bottom of the stairs.*

SEBASTIAN

(Pointing off left; sotto voice)

Soldiers! Now watch!

(He goes to the French windows, down right, and opens the iron grille.)

ESSIE

(Standing in the arch)

Rudi! What are you trying to do?

SEBASTIAN

If we can get out of here, let's run for it.

ESSIE

But you don't know who's out there or what's out there!

(She comes into the room.)

SEBASTIAN

We've got to take a chance. When we're in trouble with the act we try everything, don't we? Well, we've got to try everything now.

ESSIE

Rudi, it may be dangerous.

135

THE GREAT SEBASTIANS

SEBASTIAN
(*Deprecatingly*)
Dangerous! Oh, Essie!
> (*He opens the windows and boldly steps out. There is loud shouting and blowing of whistles. No sooner do we hear this than* SEBASTIAN *is back in the room again.*)

FIRST SOLDIER
(*Off*)
Who's that? (*The* FIRST SOLDIER *enters with pistol drawn and corners* SEBASTIAN *behind the open grille door*) What are you trying to do?
> (*The* SECOND SOLDIER *steps into the window.*)

SEBASTIAN
Just trying to get a breath of fresh air.

ESSIE
It's very close in here.
> (*The* CORPORAL *enters through the arch from the right.*)

CORPORAL
What's going on?

FIRST SOLDIER
This man came through the window. It looked as if he was trying to leave the house.

CORPORAL
(*To* SEBASTIAN)
Well, now you know you can't. (*To* FIRST SOLDIER) Good work, Novak. Go back to your posts.
> (*The two* SOLDIERS *leave, closing the French windows behind them. The* CORPORAL *crosses right, closes the grille and bolts it.*)

SEBASTIAN
As a matter of fact, we were looking for the Sergeant.

CORPORAL

What do you want with the Sergeant?

SEBASTIAN

He's had time to go through our things, hasn't he? (*The* CORPORAL *doesn't answer*) When are we going to get them back?

CORPORAL

That's up to Sergeant Javorsky.

ESSIE

(*Persuasively*)
Corporal—couldn't we just have our cigarettes back?

CORPORAL

There are cigarettes on the desk.

SEBASTIAN

We want our own cigarettes. He had no right to take them.

ESSIE

(*Going to the* CORPORAL)
Who is he? He's certainly more than just a sergeant.

CORPORAL

No, he's just a sergeant.

SEBASTIAN

Well, tonight he turned into something else—something in the Party.

ESSIE

He was being bossy to the General!

CORPORAL

(*A dawning light*)
Uh . . . Huh! . . . (*Thoughtfully*) That explains a lot!

137

ESSIE

Explains—what?

CORPORAL

He must be a political commissar. We have those in the Army, now. You don't always know who they are.

ESSIE

He tricked us. We didn't know who he was.

CORPORAL

I didn't either. It just shows you've got to be careful.
(*The* SERGEANT *enters, followed by the* THIRD SOLDIER, *who is carrying the towel containing the* SEBASTIANS' *personal effects. The* SERGEANT *has in his hand a typewritten statement. The* CORPORAL *clicks his heels and gives the* SERGEANT *a big salute, startling* ESSIE *and* SEBASTIAN *and even the* SERGEANT.)

SERGEANT JAVORSKY

What's all that about?

CORPORAL

Do you need me, sir?

SERGEANT JAVORSKY

No.

CORPORAL

Thank you, sir!
(*He gives the* SERGEANT *another extravagant salute and exits, off right. The* THIRD SOLDIER *has been placing the towel, its contents and* ESSIE'S *handbag on the upstage end of the desk.*)

SERGEANT JAVORSKY
(*To the* SEBASTIANS)

There are your things.
(*The* THIRD SOLDIER *exits, following the* CORPORAL. *The* SER-GEANT *reads to himself the statement he is carrying. The* SEBAS-

TIANS *hurry over to the desk, take a quick look for the ciga-*
rettes, which aren't there. SEBASTIAN *starts returning his things*
to his pockets. ESSIE *picks up her handbag. She stops suddenly.*)

ESSIE

Rudi, look! They've cut the lining of my bag! (*Going to the* SER-
GEANT) You've got a nerve, you have, cutting the lining of my bag!

SERGEANT JAVORSKY

Is everything there?

ESSIE
(*Muttering*)

My best evening bag—

SERGEANT JAVORSKY
(*Interrupting her*)

Is everything—

ESSIE

—I'm getting a bit fed up with you Czechs!

SEBASTIAN

Essie!

ESSIE

I wish I was out of here—!

SERGEANT JAVORSKY

Is there anything missing!

SEBASTIAN
(*Searching*)

I don't see my cigarettes!

SERGEANT JAVORSKY

They've been confiscated.
(*He returns his attention to the statement.*)

SEBASTIAN
(*Apprehensively*)

Confiscated?

SERGEANT JAVORSKY

By me, personally.

SEBASTIAN

Those cigarettes were my personal property.

SERGEANT JAVORSKY

Now they are not.

SEBASTIAN
(*A new angle*)

I was just dying for a decent smoke—

SERGEANT JAVORSKY

All right. All right.
(SEBASTIAN *crosses to the* SERGEANT *who takes the cigarette package out of his pocket, pulls out one cigarette, hands it to* SEBASTIAN, *and puts the pack back in his pocket.* SEBASTIAN *shrugs and exchanges a glance with* ESSIE. *At this moment* GENERAL ZANDEK *enters from up left, carrying his coat, hat and gloves.*)

ZANDEK
(*To* JAVORSKY)

I'm back, Comrade.
(*He throws his coat, hat and gloves on the hall bench.* ESSIE *starts returning her belongings to her handbag.*)

SERGEANT JAVORSKY

What's the situation?
(*Crosses up to* ZANDEK)

ZANDEK

All security measures have been taken. I am starting for the border as soon as I can get away.

SERGEANT JAVORSKY

Has the Prime Minister's office decided on an announcement?

ZANDEK

My understanding was they are waiting to hear from you. You were to have a statement.

SERGEANT JAVORSKY

I have it here.
(*He hands* ZANDEK *the typewritten statement and* ZANDEK *glances at it.*)

ZANDEK

It hasn't been signed.

SERGEANT JAVORSKY

Not yet.
(ZANDEK *reads the statement to himself.*)

SEBASTIAN

(*He has finished putting his effects back in his pockets*)
Can we go now?

SERGEANT JAVORSKY

Before you go, there's something I want you to do.

ESSIE

Oh? What is it?

SERGEANT JAVORSKY

I want you to sign a statement of what you know about Jan Masaryk's suicide.

ESSIE

We don't know anything about it.

SEBASTIAN

Well, if that will help, we'll be very glad to sign a statement saying we don't know anything.

SERGEANT JAVORSKY
I have had a statement prepared.

SEBASTIAN
Good. (*He pulls out the desk chair, sits and picks up the pen*) Where is it? We're in a hurry.

ESSIE
Wait a minute, Rudi—before you sign anything you've got to know what it says.

SEBASTIAN
Essie, we still have to pack.

ESSIE
Rudi, before you sign anything you've got to know what it says! Remember that contract you signed for Blackpool?

SEBASTIAN
You've got the damndest memory when you don't need it! (*To the* SERGEANT) Where is the statement?

SERGEANT JAVORSKY
The General has it.

ZANDEK
This is a good job, Comrade. I compliment you.

SEBASTIAN
Read it to us.

SERGEANT JAVORSKY
Yes, General, you read it.

ZANDEK
(*Reading the statement*)
"We, the undersigned, Rudolf Schlupp and Esther Silk Schlupp—"

SEBASTIAN

Wait a minute—where did you get those names?

SERGEANT JAVORSKY

From your passports.

ESSIE

Nosy Parker!

SEBASTIAN

We are known as the Great Sebastians.

ZANDEK

(*Repeating*)

"We, the undersigned, Rudolf Schlupp and Esther Silk Schlupp—"

SEBASTIAN

Cut out the Schlupps. Just the Great Sebastians.

ZANDEK

(*Going on*)

"—known in the music halls as the Great Sebastians, desire to reveal the conversation we had today with the late Jan Masaryk."

SEBASTIAN

(*Pleased*)

Oh, is this for the newspapers?

SERGEANT JAVORSKY

Yes—for all over the world.

SEBASTIAN

That's good. Oh, Essie, that's good! Go ahead.

ZANDEK

(*Reading*)

"We became acquainted with Mr. Masaryk in London, during World War II, when he was a member there of the Czechoslovakian

Government in Exile. We worked with him on broadcasts to the resistance movement in Czechoslovakia."

ESSIE
(Interrupting)
I think you should say our acquaintance was not just business— we were friends, as well.

SEBASTIAN
And you might add we were frequent visitors at the Masaryk apartment.

ZANDEK
(Reading)
"This was the last day of our engagement at the Théâtre Variété in Prague. At Mr. Masaryk's invitation, we had lunch with him this noon in his apartment in Czernin Palace."

ESSIE
There were just the three of us.

SEBASTIAN
Nobody else.

ESSIE
Quite private.

ZANDEK
(Reading)
"We found him in a serious state of depression."

SEBASTIAN
No. No. We didn't say that. We said he was quiet, but not depressed. You'll have to change that.

SERGEANT JAVORSKY
(Steps toward SEBASTIAN)
I suggest that you be quiet! Go on, General.

ZANDEK
(*Reading*)
"After lunch he said he wanted to take us into his confidence. He confessed that he felt he had betrayed the people of Czechoslovakia."

SEBASTIAN

Ach!
(*Surprised and shocked, he can only stare and listen.*)

ZANDEK
(*Reading*)
"He told us that because of his long residence in the West, especially England, he had lost all sense of social values and human justice —that he now realized that only under communism can the people of Czechoslovakia find happiness, prosperity and peace."

SEBASTIAN
But he didn't say anything like that!

SERGEANT JAVORSKY
Quiet!

SEBASTIAN
(*Rising*)
I tell you he didn't say anything like that!

SERGEANT JAVORSKY
(*Silencing him*)
Let him finish! (SEBASTIAN *sits*. SERGEANT JAVORSKY *goes to* ZANDEK) Go on.

ZANDEK
(*Reading*)
"He said he realized he had worked against the best interests of Czechoslovakia, that he had betrayed his country, his countrymen, and the very name of Masaryk. It is clear to us now that it was for these reasons Jan Masaryk committed suicide."

SEBASTIAN

But he didn't say anything like that!

SERGEANT JAVORSKY

That has nothing to do with it. (*He takes the paper from* ZANDEK, *crosses above* ESSIE, *dips the pen in the ink and offers it to her*) Madame, you will sign first.

ESSIE

(*Ignoring the pen*)

Me sign that? Why, that's just a pack of lies. Sign it yourself—you made it up! Don't get me mixed up in a thing like that. That's crooked!

SERGEANT JAVORSKY

This statement is in the interest of the People's Democracy! (*He puts the paper and pen on the desk, in front of* ESSIE.)

ESSIE

That's what you think. I'd like to know what they think. Or don't you allow them to think?

SEBASTIAN

Madame—

ESSIE

(*Ignoring* SEBASTIAN)

The People's Democracy! (*Turning to the* SERGEANT) You don't give a tuppenny damn about the people.

SEBASTIAN

(*Obviously trying code*)

Madame, don't you remember—

ESSIE

(*To the* SERGEANT)

If you're going to lie, do it off your own bat! Don't get nice, decent people into a thing like that!

SEBASTIAN

Madame—

ESSIE

(*Turning on* SEBASTIAN)
Don't madame me! This is no time for it.

SEBASTIAN

Madame, don't you remember?

ESSIE

No, I don't remember. Whose side are you on?

SEBASTIAN

(*Angrily*)
Whose side do you think I'm on?
    (ESSIE *shuts up.*)

ZANDEK

Comrade Javorsky, let me talk to them.

SERGEANT JAVORSKY

(*Curtly*)
You keep out of this. This is a Party matter.

ESSIE

(*Rising, crossing down left*)
A nice party this has turned out to be.
    (ZANDEK, *rebuffed, exits up the stairs.* ESSIE *sits in a chair,
    down left.*)

SERGEANT JAVORSKY

(*Trying quiet tactics*)
You plan on leaving Prague this morning by train?

SEBASTIAN

Yes.

147

SERGEANT JAVORSKY

You're returning to England?

SEBASTIAN

Yes.

SERGEANT JAVORSKY

Your children are in England. Those were their pictures I found in your wallet?

SEBASTIAN
(*Disturbed for the first time*)

Yes—

SERGEANT JAVORSKY

You must want to see your children. And if you want to see your children—(*Pleasantly*)—if I were you, I'd sign the statement.

SEBASTIAN

And if we don't sign?

SERGEANT JAVORSKY

We'll have to keep you here.

SEBASTIAN

Here in this house?

SERGEANT JAVORSKY
(*Crossing to him*)

For people who will not work with us, we have—other places.

ESSIE
(*Calmly*)

Hark at the bogey man. We're ever so frightened.

SERGEANT JAVORSKY

It might be wise of you to be frightened! Both of you!
(ESSIE'S *back is turned to* SEBASTIAN, *who rises and pantomimes to the* SERGEANT *to leave.*)

148

SERGEANT JAVORSKY

I'll let you think it over.
(*He goes to the arch.*)

ESSIE

I've thought it over.

SEBASTIAN

Madame, may I have your attention—

SERGEANT JAVORSKY

I'll be back in five minutes.

ESSIE

You needn't come back, it won't do you any good.

SEBASTIAN

(*Doggedly*)
Madame, will you give me your attention—

SERGEANT JAVORSKY

I've left the statement there.
(*Indicating the desk, he turns and starts out right.*)

ESSIE

(*Rising and calling after him*)
You can take it with you, and you know what you can do with it!

SEBASTIAN

Essie!
(*The* SERGEANT *is off.*)

ESSIE

(*As* SEBASTIAN *hurries and closes the sliding doors*)
What the hell were you trying to say to me!

SEBASTIAN

I was trying to say go slow—go slow. I've got an idea.

ESSIE

(*Still angry*)

What idea?

SEBASTIAN

Let's sign the paper and get out of here—get out of Czechoslovakia. (*Going back to the desk.*)

ESSIE

Rudi! I thought you had a sense of decency. Jan Masaryk was your friend.

SEBASTIAN

Essie, let me finish, will you?

ESSIE

And now you're willing to put lies in his mouth?

SEBASTIAN

No, I'm not!

ESSIE

Now that he's dead and can't deny them!

SEBASTIAN

Damn it, let me talk a minute—let me finish. You haven't heard what I'm going to say.

ESSIE

What are you going to say?

SEBASTIAN

The minute we get out of Czechoslovakia, we can tell the truth. We can deny every word of that statement.

ESSIE

That's your brilliant idea.

SEBASTIAN

Now, Essie. (*He sits in the desk chair*) We're booked to open in Brighton on the twenty-first.

ESSIE

To hell with Brighton.

SEBASTIAN

(*Shocked*)

Essie! The Great Sebastians have never missed a booking! You've got to think of the act.

ESSIE

To hell with the act!

SEBASTIAN

Essie!

ESSIE

Do you want to sign that paper?

SEBASTIAN

Why, no! But our contract with the circuit calls for fourteen weeks —it's play or pay!

ESSIE

All right . . . we'll pay.
(*There is a moment of silence.* SEBASTIAN *rises slowly.*)

SEBASTIAN

This is a side of you I've never seen before!

ESSIE

This is a side of you I've never seen before.

SEBASTIAN

Essie, what's wrong with signing the statement now and telling the truth when we get across the border?

ESSIE

What about this side of the border?

SEBASTIAN

What about it?

ESSIE

The only Czech who would know the truth would be you! That Sergeant and his gang wouldn't let the truth get back here—the people who love Masaryk are here—and all they'd ever be told would be that pack of lies with our names on it! I'd rather go to jail than sign that paper. (*She turns away and then turns back to* SEBASTIAN) I'm not being a bloody angel, Rudi—I know we've done a bit of hanky-panky in our time—but this is different. This isn't income tax, you know—putting in more expenses than we really had—(*Moving across the room*)—this isn't getting something tasty on the black market. This is serious. (*On the verge of tears*) I don't understand you, Rudi. . . .(*She sinks down on a chair, stage left, and takes her handkerchief out of her purse. She is deeply moved*) Mr. Masaryk was sweet to you. He was sweet to both of us—he was a sweet man. And now you're willing to put lies in his mouth, now that he's dead and can't deny them. . . . (SEBASTIAN *goes to her*). . . I'm ashamed of you, I am. A fine friend you are . . .

(*She turns away from him, her handkerchief to her mouth.*)

SEBASTIAN

(*Standing behind her, trying to comfort her*)

No, no, you're right, Essie. This is serious. We've just never had to face up to anything like this before. This is big. This is a big thing. My God—this is bigger than the act . . . ! I'm proud of you, Essie, I really am.

ESSIE

Proud of me—what for?

SEBASTIAN

You didn't even have to think to know what we had to do.

(*He goes to the desk, picks up the statement and tears it in half.* ESSIE *watches this with a sudden trepidation.*)

ESSIE

Rudi . . . do you think we'll be what they call—liquidated?

SEBASTIAN

That always sounded to me like being put in a bottle.

(*He returns and sits beside her.*)

ESSIE

We'd make a fine pair of vases on the mantelpiece. . . .
(*She laughs weakly at her own joke, but the laughter is close to tears.* SEBASTIAN *puts his arm around her.*)

SEBASTIAN

Whatever happens, we'll be together.

ESSIE

In this world anyway.

SEBASTIAN

And the next!

ESSIE

Do you really believe that, Rudi?

SEBASTIAN

Why, yes, I do. I just can't believe that we would close here and not open somewhere else.
(*He kisses her tenderly on her shoulder. They sit there for a moment, contemplating eternity. Then an idea occurs to* SEBASTIAN. *He rises, thinks for a second longer, then with decision crosses to the desk and sits. He takes some paper and begins writing.* ESSIE *is not conscious of this.*)

ESSIE

Oh! Edie was going to be at Northold to meet our plane Monday. (SEBASTIAN *is concentrating on his writing endeavor*) Do you think they'll let us wire her to say we've been delayed? (SEBASTIAN *doesn't look up*) I do think we ought to tell her not to put off the wedding. (*She is a little tearful, now*) I do—hate—to miss the wedding. . . . (*She turns to him. Her tears change to curiosity*) Whatever are you doing?

SEBASTIAN

(*Resisting interruption, struggling with the act of creation*)
I'm writing.

153

ESSIE

To Chris and Edie?

SEBASTIAN

(*Continuing writing*)
No—to the newspapers—a press release.

ESSIE

What about?

SEBASTIAN

About us.

ESSIE

Oh, Rudi! These papers here won't publish anything about us—
especially now.

SEBASTIAN

No, no, I don't mean the papers here. (*Looking up before him*)
Essie, what was the name of that little press agent in Finsbury Park—
the one who named his baby after you? He'd do anything for us.

ESSIE

What's he got to do with it?

SEBASTIAN

Well, if somehow we could get this to him, he could get it pub-
lished all over England—maybe even in America. You know, I've
always wanted to play America.

ESSIE

(*Rising and going slowly to him*)
I'd understand you better if you gave it to me in code. Even if it
was the new code.

SEBASTIAN

Essie, don't you realize we're being noble? We're being pretty
damned noble! Well, if we're being this noble, we ought to get bill-
ing!

ESSIE

Rudi! We're not doing this to get our names in the paper!

SEBASTIAN

When did getting our names in the paper ever do us any harm?

ESSIE

Rudi!

SEBASTIAN

Listen, we're setting a good example. How can we set a good example unless people know about it?

ESSIE

Give me that! (*She takes the paper, crumples it, and throws it in wastepaper basket*) You don't act decent to set an example—you act decent because you are!

SEBASTIAN

You never did understand the value of publicity
       (*He rises.*)

ESSIE

Not that kind. I'll say one thing for Alexander—He would never have done a thing like that—and he did plenty. He even bloodied my nose once.

SEBASTIAN

That's the first thing I ever heard about Alexander that I could admire!

ESSIE

Listen, if you had the brains Alexander had, we wouldn't be in this fix!

SEBASTIAN

Hark at you! How did we get in this fix? Back in the dressing room, when the General said to the Sergeant, "Quickly," you blurted out "key!"

ESSIE

"Quickly" is your code word for key!

SEBASTIAN

And that was the first and probably the last time you'll ever get it right.

ESSIE

If you hadn't changed Alexander's code—and we're going back to it—

SEBASTIAN

(*Turning away*)

Never!

(*The* SERGEANT *and* CORPORAL *push the sliding doors open and enter.*)

ESSIE

—we're going back—(*Seeing the* SERGEANT, *turning her anger on him*)—to our hotel if you don't mind!

(*The* SERGEANT *goes to the desk, picks up the torn halves of the statement.*)

SERGEANT JAVORSKY

Your hotel tonight will be Pankrac Prison! (*He throws the torn halves on desk, crosses up to the* CORPORAL) Keep them here. Tell General Zandek that when I get to headquarters I will have Security send for them. (*The* CORPORAL *exits up the stairs. The* SERGEANT *turns to the* SEBASTIANS) You will stay at Pankrac until—it will be up to you to decide how long.

(*He goes up into the arch.*)

ESSIE

(*Following him*)

That will be the first Tuesday after hell freezes over!

SERGEANT JAVORSKY

(*Curtly*)

Good night; Good night, Madame. You are a stubborn British bitch!

(*He exits, off left.*)

ESSIE

(*Swings up into the arch, calls after him*)
I'm glad I'm stubborn!

SEBASTIAN

(*Follows the* SERGEANT *quickly into the hall, looks off, after him, turns back to* ESSIE)
I'm glad you're British! Essie! Have you got your registration card from the British Consulate?

ESSIE

Yes. It's in my bag.
(*She starts to search her bag.*)

SEBASTIAN

Has it got the telephone number on it?

ESSIE

Why?

SEBASTIAN

You heard what he called you—"stubborn British—"

ESSIE

That's not all he called me.

SEBASTIAN

(*Going to the desk*)
Essie, the British Government isn't going to let these damn Czechs do this to us—(*Examining the wires of the telephone*) Now, if they haven't cut off the telephone—

ESSIE

Rudi, they aren't that stupid.

SEBASTIAN

Listen, I told you we have to try everything, didn't I?
(*He reaches gingerly for the telephone.*)

THE GREAT SEBASTIANS

ESSIE

(*Remembering his experience with the* SOLDIERS *in the garden*)
I hope it doesn't whistle at you.

SEBASTIAN

(*Withdraws his hand nervously as she speaks, then gets up the
courage to pick up the receiver; he listens a second*)
It's alive!
   (*Hangs up again.*)

ESSIE

(*Handing him the card from her bag*)
Here it is—there's the number!

SEBASTIAN

(*Indicating the arch*)
Essie—stand guard. Watch out for that Corporal. He's upstairs.

ESSIE

Rudi, you're marvelous! Alexander would never have thought of
this. (*She pats him on the back and goes to the arch. The favorable
comparison with Alexander so stuns* SEBASTIAN *that he cannot even
reach for the telephone. He sits motionless with a look of happy in-
credulity.* ESSIE *goes part way up the stairs where she can watch both
upper and lower floors. Hearing nothing from him, she looks toward*
SEBASTIAN) What's the matter—don't they answer? Rudi, make it fast!

SEBASTIAN

(*Comes out of his daze and dials feverishly. After a moment he
speaks into the telephone*)
Yes? Who is it? Oh, Mr. Secretary. I'm very sorry to disturb you
at this time of night, but it's a matter of great importance. My wife
and I—(*Pause*) Oh, yes, of course. I should have told you. This is
Sebastian of the Great Sebastians. (*Pause*)—Sebastian of the Great
Sebastians. (*Pause*) Listen, I have told you twice! Sebastian of the
Great Sebastians! We're a headline act. We've been playing the
Variété. (*Pause*) Well, where is your home? We've played every
theatre in England. (*Pause*) We broke the house record in Notting-

ham. Six months ago we broke the house record at the Palladium in London. (*Pause*) Were you in London six months ago? The Palladium? (*Pause*) Well, of course you remember the mind-reading act! (*Pause*) We broke the house record. (*Pause*) Well perhaps you would remember it better this way—there was an American on the bill with us—his name was Danny Kaye.

ESSIE
(*Comes down the stairs and into the room*)
Rudi, never mind telling him who we are. Tell him we're being held here! Tell him they've got to do something about it!
(*She returns to the hall and stands guard.*)

SEBASTIAN
(*Into the telephone*)
We're—we're—we're being held prisoners here—my wife and I—(*Pause*) Here in Prague! (*Cupping his hand over the receiver*) At General Zandek's house! . . . (*Pause*) Well I'll tell you what it has to do with you! My wife is a British subject—She's registered at your Consulate! . . . Well, look! (*Pause*) Ach! . . . Her name on the registery, would be under—Esther . . . Silk . . . Schlupp . . . S-C-H-L-U-P-P. (*Pause*) But the name of the act is the Great Sebastians. Hello? . . . Hello? . . . (*He hangs up. He is close to tears*) Essie . . . He never heard of the act.

ESSIE
(*Coming down to him*)
Never mind, Rudi. . . . Well, I suppose we're in for it.
(*She sits.*)

SEBASTIAN
(*At his lowest low*)
I'm sorry, Essie. . . . But when they find out in England that we're being held here, there'll be hell to pay!

ESSIE
If they find out. It may be a year or more before anybody knows.

SEBASTIAN

Listen, if Harry Wilson doesn't miss us before then, he's a lousy agent.

(GENERAL ZANDEK *comes quickly down the stairs and into the room.*)

ZANDEK

I have just heard. They are taking you to Pankrac Prison. Do you know that?

SEBASTIAN

Yes, we know.

ZANDEK

You are very foolish people. Why don't you sign that statement. They will make you sign it when you get there. You will find out.

ESSIE

I'd like to see them try.

ZANDEK

They will start the minute you get to Pankrac. The questions—before you go to sleep tonight—tomorrow—the next day—hour after hour. They won't let you sleep until you sign.

ESSIE

What's it to you whether we sign or not?

ZANDEK

Let me call Comrade Javorsky. Let me tell him I have talked to you—that you will sign.

SEBASTIAN

So that's it.

ZANDEK

That's what?

SEBASTIAN

You think that if you can get us to sign, it will get you in right with the Sergeant.

ZANDEK

What did you say? What do you know?

SEBASTIAN

You wanted to find out who was disloyal—Well, you've found out!

ZANDEK

Did Javorsky say anything? Did he talk about me? Was he in this house to spy on me? Tell me!

ESSIE

We're not fortune tellers.

ZANDEK

You are mind readers—you say you are mind readers! Tonight in your dressing room, you read Javorsky's mind. I saw it myself. That's why I brought you here. Tell me what is on his mind now.

ESSIE

He doesn't happen to be here.

ZANDEK

What difference does that make? People miles from each other sometimes are thinking of the same thing. If you can read minds— read his—read his now!

ESSIE

You go and be a general somewhere else.

ZANDEK

(Straightening up; indignant)

Ach! . . . You are not only charlatans, you are fools. (Going to the arch) You are fools not to sign that statement. Your names on a piece of paper, and you could go—you've got the chance to get out of the country—if I were in your place— (*He turns and goes up the stairs, still talking*)—Why should I waste my breath on you—you fools—you idiots—you imbeciles—you won't listen to reason—

(*He is out of sight.* SEBASTIAN *has risen and crossed up to the arch, watching* ZANDEK *as he has gone up the stairs.* ESSIE *has joined him.*)

SEBASTIAN

(*Turning to* ESSIE *in an excited half-whisper*)
He's got the wind up!

ESSIE

Did you hear what he said? Did you hear what he said?

SEBASTIAN

He's frightened of the Sergeant! Essie, if we only knew how frightened—

ESSIE

He said, "If I were in your place—"

SEBASTIAN

(*Busy with his own thoughts*)
Essie, he's our best bet. He's scared! He's scared of what's going to happen to him!

ESSIE

(*Thinking aloud*)
"—If I were in your place."

SEBASTIAN

We can break him—I know we can break him. But we've got to think! We've got to think how!

ESSIE

(*Still following her own thought*)
Rudi, is there such a thing as a subconscious mind?
(*She sits in chair left of the desk.*)

162

SEBASTIAN

What have we still got on him? Lost in the forest—what was it his mother called him?

(*He sits in a chair down left.*)

ESSIE

We're always talking about a subconscious mind. Is that just to impress people or *is* there one?

SEBASTIAN

What?

ESSIE

Is there such a thing as a subconscious mind—and if there is, what is it?

SEBASTIAN

It's where you think but you don't know you're thinking. Now. When the General comes back—

ESSIE

(*Excitedly*)

I've just read one, I think. I know I have! I've just read the General's subconscious mind! Rudi, I am a mind reader!

SEBASTIAN

(*Rising and pacing*)

Essie, this is no time to come down with delusions of grandeur!

ESSIE

Didn't you hear him say—

SEBASTIAN

(*Sits again*)

Yes, I heard everything he said. Now just pull yourself together—

THE GREAT SEBASTIANS

ESSIE

(*Interrupting*)

He said, "You've got a chance to get out of the country. If I were in your place . . ." That means that in his subconscious mind—he wants to get out of the country!

SEBASTIAN

Essie, if you can just hold on till—What did you say?

ESSIE

He wants to get out of the country!
(SEBASTIAN *stands and opens his arms.*)

SEBASTIAN

Essie! Kiss me! (*He crosses to her as* ESSIE *rises, and they meet in an embrace*) You're right! That's how scared he is!

ESSIE

How can we use it?

SEBASTIAN

It's the Sergeant he's scared of!

ESSIE

If I'd only known this when he asked me to read the Sergeant's mind. I would have read the Sergeant's mind for him!

SEBASTIAN

Well, perhaps you still can. That's the one mind the General believes you can read.

ZANDEK

(*Off, at the top of the stairs*)

Put that in the car.

SEBASTIAN

(*To* ESSIE)

Here! (*He indicates the chair to the left of the desk. She sits. He sits on the edge of the desk upstage of her*) Project, Madame, project!

ESSIE

Where is he? . . . Where is he? . . .
(*She has gone into her trance. The* CORPORAL *comes down the stairs.*)

SEBASTIAN

Find him, Madame, find him—

ZANDEK
(*Off*)

Corporal!

CORPORAL
(*Stops, looks back up the stairs*)

Yes, sir!
(ZANDEK *comes into view on the stairs.*)

ESSIE

He's there somewhere—

ZANDEK
(*To* CORPORAL *as they come down the stairs*)
Tell Franta it will be a long trip. Be sure he has enough petrol.

SEBASTIAN

Keep searching, Madame. . . .
(*The* CORPORAL *exits, left.*)

ESSIE

. . . He's closer—he's closer—

ZANDEK
(*Now in the hall, calling off*)
When he's ready let me know.

CORPORAL
(*Off*)

Yes, sir.

SEBASTIAN

Hurry, Madame, hurry.
 (ZANDEK *exits, off right*.)

ESSIE

There he is . . . I've found him. I've found the Sergeant!

SEBASTIAN
 (*Looking around*)
Never mind, you've lost the General. (*He gets up, crosses to the arch, looks off right*) He's gone.

ESSIE

Gone? (*Springing up*) Out of the house?
 (*Joining* SEBASTIAN.)

SEBASTIAN
 (*Indicating*)
No—that way. He left his hat and coat.

ESSIE

Then he has to come back for them!

SEBASTIAN

We've got to work fast. We've got to watch for a break. Now if either of us sees the slightest opening—remember "surely."

ESSIE

"Surely?"

SEBASTIAN

Well you haven't forgotten "surely"—you know what "surely" means—it means we've got a hint, a clue—pick it up—go to work on it!

ESSIE
 (*Eyeing him balefully*)
"Surely" is the old code.

166

SEBASTIAN
(*Resignedly*)
Essie, we're in trouble . . . We'll go back to the old code.

ESSIE
(*Going back to the chair and sitting*)
Now you're talking! Now, I'm ready for anything.

SEBASTIAN
(*Looking off right*)
Well, here comes something. Project, Madame— (*He quickly goes
back to his seated position on the edge of the desk*) Project—
(ESSIE *goes into her "trance" again staring directly forward.*
GENERAL ZANDEK *comes into hall from off right and starts
putting on his overcoat.*)

ESSIE
I see something moving. It's a car. It's moving. . . .
(ZANDEK *glances into the room.*)

SEBASTIAN
Is he in the car, Madame?

ESSIE
There are two men in the car.

SEBASTIAN
Is he one of them? Can you reach his mind?
(ZANDEK *becomes curious.*)

ESSIE
Yes. It is he—it is the Sergeant. (ZANDEK *comes slowly into the room*)
He's angry at someone. . . . It's a cold anger. . . .

SEBASTIAN
Can you hear what he is saying? We must know what he's planning
to do with us. Try, Madame, try! . . .

ESSIE

He's saying . . . "Let him think himself safe. . . . Next week . . . next week. . . ." Now it's fading. Something's interfering.

SEBASTIAN
(Desperately)

Try again, Madame. Surely you can find him again. . . . Surely! Surely!

ESSIE

I can't find him. . . . Oh, now I see something moving—it's not a car—it's a boy—it's a child. He's in a forest. He's frightened. He's lost. . . . He's lost in a forest.

ZANDEK
(Awed, moving in behind ESSIE)

I . . . was lost in a forest. . . .

ESSIE

Now he's running. . . . Now he's standing still. Now he's listening. I hear a voice . . . calling—"Pepi! Pepi!"

ZANDEK
(Leaning toward ESSIE)

My mother! . . . That was my mother! No one called me Pepi but my mother! . . . Why should my mother be in my mind?

ESSIE
(Still in her "trance" voice)

In the forest you were frightened.

ZANDEK

Yes. I was frightened. She found me.

ESSIE

She will always find you when you are frightened. You are frightened now. You think to escape—to leave the country!

ZANDEK

No! No! That is not in my mind.

ESSIE

It was in your mind.

ZANDEK

No. I am loyal. I am a loyal member of the Party! It is not in my mind!

SEBASTIAN

It was in your mind, you can't deny it. It was in your mind.

ZANDEK

For a moment only!
(ESSIE *snaps out of her "trance" and they both rise and turn to* ZANDEK.)

ESSIE and SEBASTIAN

Ah! . . .

ZANDEK

The thought just crossed my mind! I put it right out!

SEBASTIAN

Until you escape, it will never be out of your mind.

ZANDEK
(*To* SEBASTIAN)

No—that is not true!

SEBASTIAN

Remember, General . . . "rhinoceros!"

ZANDEK
(*Capitulating*)

You are right. It will never be out of my mind now. It was when they mentioned the border, that the thought first came to me: "If I can get to the border—I can get across."

SEBASTIAN

And you will take us with you.

ZANDEK

Impossible!

SEBASTIAN

Then we will take you to Pankrac with us. Surely we will.

ESSIE

We're not important, General, but *you* . . . when they find out about *you* (*Echoing* ZANDEK's *own words*). . . . the questions—before you go to sleep tonight—tomorrow—the next day—hour after hour. . . .

ZANDEK

Wait! Wait! I will try.

CORPORAL

(*Off, left*)

I will tell him you are here!

ZANDEK

(*Raising his voice*)

Who is it?

CORPORAL

(*Entering, comes to attention in the hall*)

Corporal Kozak, sir. Your chauffeur is here with the car.

ZANDEK

(*Going to him*)

Tell him to wait! (*The* CORPORAL *exits, left.* ZANDEK *comes back into the room, in thought*) Look. (*He goes to grilled window*) At the end of the garden there is a path which leads to a gate—a small green gate. It opens onto the river road. (*Making a sweeping gesture with his right arm*) I will drive my car around and meet you there. We will have to act quickly, before they come for you! I will start now.

(*He starts for the arch.*)

SEBASTIAN

General— (*Stopping* ZANDEK) We don't like tricks, you know.

ZANDEK

This is no trick—I promise you!

SEBASTIAN

A half-hour ago I tried to get out of that window. All hell broke loose. I damn near got shot!

ZANDEK

Of course—they are my bodyguards. They are on duty only when I am here. (*He crosses to the grille and opens it*) I will take care of them immediately!

ESSIE

What about your chauffeur?

ZANDEK

(*Opening the French windows*)

He is an animal—a dog. He will do what I tell him. (*Calling off*) Novak! Salda! (*He comes back into the room. The* FIRST *and* SECOND SOLDIERS *enter through the window and come to attention*) I am leaving for the border immediately. You are relieved of duty. Report to your barracks. Tell Captain Burian I expect to return tomorrow at six. You will report here at five.

FIRST SOLDIER

Very good, sir.

ZANDEK

You may go!

(*The* SOLDIERS *start for the arch, and are about to exit when suddenly they step back on either side of the arch and snap to attention.* SERGEANT JAVORSKY *comes into the arch from off left, throws his coat on the bench and strides into the room. Behind him are two* SECURITY POLICEMEN. *They stop in front of the bench and face into the room.*)

ZANDEK

Javorsky!

SERGEANT JAVORSKY

(*To* ZANDEK)

How did the British Consulate find out these people were being
held here?

ZANDEK

It's impossible! How could they know!

SERGEANT JAVORSKY

(*Turning to* ESSIE)

I suppose, Madame, they read your mind all the way from Nerdova
Street! (*He looks at the telephone, crosses to it, picks it up and yanks
the wire loose from the floor. He takes the phone and speaks to*
ESSIE *as he crosses upstage center*) The relations between the People's
Democracy and the British Government have been strained—but
fortunately for you, not to the breaking point.

(*He hands the telephone to the* FIRST SECURITY POLICEMAN, *who
puts it on the hall bench.*)

ESSIE

Oh?

SERGEANT JAVORSKY

The Foreign Office has instructed me to inform you that you are
—free.

(*He has taken out* SEBASTIAN'S *package of cigarettes and removed one.*)

SEBASTIAN

Good. Then I can have back my cigarettes.

(*He goes quickly to* JAVORSKY.)

SERGEANT JAVORSKY

I'm sorry. This is the last one. (*He crumples the package in his
hand, glances around for a place to put it, throws it in the ash tray
on the table down left.* ESSIE'S *and* SEBASTIAN'S *eyes follow it*) I'm
afraid I owe you a package of cigarettes.

SEBASTIAN

I'm afraid you owe us a great deal more than that (*He looks toward the crumpled package and decides to accept a financial loss, as he moves toward the arch.* ESSIE, *however, is gravitating toward the crumpled package*) Come on, Essie, we barely have time to make our train.

(ESSIE *is in the act of reaching for the crumpled package when* JAVORSKY's *next speech stops her.*)

SERGEANT JAVORSKY

Madame! You wish to get out of the country. You shall, as soon as we can arrange it.

ZANDEK

(*Going to* JAVORSKY)

Comrade Javorsky, I am leaving for the border this minute. I could put her across the border myself. I'll be glad to.

SERGEANT JAVORSKY

Good! Do it. As far as I'm concerned, you can kick her across.

SEBASTIAN

Not while I'm there!

SERGEANT JAVORSKY

(*Going to* SEBASTIAN)

You—won't be there! You are a Czech. You will remain in Czechoslovakia!

ESSIE

Then I won't go! I refuse to go! (*She rushes to* SEBASTIAN) We've never been separated!

SERGEANT JAVORSKY

That's enough!

(*He pulls* ESSIE *away from* SEBASTIAN)

173

SEBASTIAN

Take your hands off her! I'll knock your teeth in.
(*He knocks the* SERGEANT *to the floor, down left. The two* SOLDIERS *rush to seize* SEBASTIAN, *as the* SECURITY POLICEMEN *come in, take* ESSIE *and pull her back to the arch.*)

ESSIE

Take your hands off me! Leave me be! (ESSIE *is struggling with the* SECURITY POLICEMEN, SEBASTIAN *with the* SOLDIERS) Let him go! Let him go!
(*The* SERGEANT *has got to his feet.*)

SEBASTIAN

No—Essie, don't! Please don't! It won't do any good!

SECOND SOLDIER

(*To* SEBASTIAN, *who has ceased to struggle*)
What do you think you're doing!

FIRST SOLDIER

Don't try anything like that around here!

SERGEANT JAVORSKY

(*Going to the* SECOND SECURITY POLICEMAN)
Your handcuffs! (*The* SECOND SECURITY POLICEMAN, *holding* ESSIE *with his right hand, takes handcuffs out of his overcoat pocket and hands them to the* SERGEANT) They're locked! Where's the key? (*The* SECURITY POLICEMAN *pulls a key, attached to a ten-inch white ribbon, out of his left-hand breast pocket, hands it to the* SERGEANT, *who turns and addresses the* SOLDIERS) Bring him over!
(*He crosses to the opened grille door.*)

SECOND SOLDIER

(*To* SEBASTIAN)
Come on, come on—quit stalling!

THE GREAT SEBASTIANS

ESSIE
(*As the* SOLDIERS *literally drag* SEBASTIAN *across the stage*)
I won't go, Rudi! I won't leave you! They can't make me go!
(*The* SERGEANT *is now downstage of the opened grille. As*
SEBASTIAN *is dragged over to the grille, the* FIRST SOLDIER *has
his right arm, the* SECOND, *his left. They halt* SEBASTIAN *to face
the grille.*)

SERGEANT JAVORSKY
(*To* FIRST SOLDIER)
Hold out his arm! Hold it still. Now lift it up. Higher! Hold it
there.
(*He snaps one handcuff around* SEBASTIAN'S *right wrist, then
the other to the top of the iron grille door. He stuffs the key
into his right breast pocket, with the ribbon hanging out.*)

ESSIE
You have no right to do this! (*To* SEBASTIAN) If they're going to
keep you here, they've got to keep me too!

SEBASTIAN
(*Seeing the ribbon hanging out of the* SERGEANT'S *pocket*)
Go quickly, Essie! Do you hear me?—Quickly!—Quickly! Quickly!—
(*We cannot tell from* ESSIE'S *behavior whether she has recog-
nized the code or not. The* SERGEANT *goes to below the desk.*)

ESSIE
(*Struggling down center*)
You can't do this to us! You can't do this! (*The* FIRST SECURITY
POLICEMAN *twists her arm behind her; she cries out as if in pain*)
Ohhh! Ohhhhh! . . .

ESSIE
(*Still groaning, she pretends to grow faint*)
Let me sit down! . . . (*The* SECURITY POLICEMEN *allow her to sit
in the chair beside the desk, and release her arms. No sooner is she
free than she jumps up and tips the chair over, causing the* SECURITY
POLICEMEN, *as they grab for her, to sprawl on the floor. She reaches*

the SERGEANT, *attacks him, hysterically beating on his chest*) You've done this! You've done this! You liar! You sneak—you stool pigeon! (*She brings the nails of her left hand down the* SERGEANT'S *cheek. He holds her hands against his chest as they struggle.*)

SERGEANT JAVORSKY

Get her away from me! Get her away from me! (*The* SECURITY POLICEMEN *scramble to their feet, seize* ESSIE *again and start leading her toward the arch. To the* SECURITY POLICEMEN) No, wait. (*They stop.* ESSIES's *back is to the footlights; she is bent over, her hands to her face*) Madame, what happens to your husband depends on you— what you say—and what you don't say!

ESSIE
(*Straightening up, turning her head to the* SERGEANT)
I will cause no trouble. . . . I will go with the General—if you will let me kiss my husband good-bye. (*The* SERGEANT *looks at her, pauses, then gestures the permission.* ESSIE *is led to* SEBASTIAN, *and, with her arms held outstretched by the* SECURITY POLICEMEN, *is allowed to kiss* SEBASTIAN—*long and tenderly*) . . . Surely I will see you again, Rudi—*Surely* . . .

SERGEANT JAVORSKY
(*Picking up* ESSIE's *handbag from the desk*)
General, get her out of here.

ZANDEK
(*Crossing to the* SERGEANT, *he takes the handbag; to the* SECURITY POLICEMEN)
Put her in my car.
(ESSIE *exits up and off left, still held by the two* SECURITY POLICEMEN, *and followed by the two* SOLDIERS *and* GENERAL ZANDEK. SEBASTIAN *collapses against the grille. The* SERGEANT *crosses to him and makes sure that he is still securely fastened to the grille.*)

SERGEANT JAVORSKY
I will be back with another copy of the statement for you to sign. You will sign it.

THE GREAT SEBASTIANS

(He goes to arch, exits off right. Gradually, SEBASTIAN's *head comes up. He turns toward the arch. He steps as far from the window as the handcuffs will permit, looking toward the arch and listening. He draws himself up. He is* THE GREAT SEBASTIAN. *The thumb and forefinger of his left hand reach into his mouth. He slowly pulls out the length of narrow white ribbon, with the key at its end. He returns the end of the ribbon to his teeth, holding it there while he runs his fingers down the ribbon and takes hold of the key. He unlocks the handcuff from his wrist. He looks back toward the arch, then quickly exits through the open windows. Several seconds elapse before he suddenly comes hurtling back through them, runs across the room to where the crumpled cigarette package still lies, picks up the package and, smoothing it out, looks inside as he moves back toward the French windows. His face lights up. He throws a good-bye salute toward the arch, slips through the open windows and disappears.)*

Curtain